Grand Duchess Elena Pavlovna, Princess Isabel and the Ending of Servile Labour in Russia and Brazil

Shane O'Rourke

ANTHEM PRESS

Anthem Press
An imprint of Wimbledon Publishing Company
www.anthempress.com

This edition was first published in UK and USA 2023
by ANTHEM PRESS
75–76 Blackfriars Road, London SE1 8HA, UK
or PO Box 9779, London SW19 7ZG, UK
and
244 Madison Ave #116, New York, NY 10016, USA

British Library Cataloguing-in-Publication Data
A catalogue record for this book is available from the British Library.

Library of Congress Cataloging-in-Publication Data
A catalog record for this book has been requested.
2023936185

ISBN-13: 978-1-83998-316-0 (pbk)
ISBN-10: 1-83998-316-7 (pbk)

Cover Credit: Grand Duchess Elena Pavlovna of Russia, née Fredericke Charlotte
of Wurrtemburg from Wikimedia commons {{PD-USGov-Congress}}.

This title is also available as an e-book.

For my teachers in Ukraine: Olena Ionkina and Kateryna Minakova

For I recalled that many landowners in Russia do not work for themselves; and therefore in many regions of Russia the productivity of the land demonstrates the oppressed lot of its inhabitants. My pleasure changed to indignation comparable to my feelings when in the summertime I walk on the pier at the customs station, gazing on the ships that transport to us America's surpluses and her expensive products, like sugar, coffee, pigments and other items in which the sweat, tears and blood drenching them during their production have yet to dry out.

(Alexander Radishchev, *Journey from St. Petersburg to Moscow*)

Wherever one studies it, slavery passes over the territory and peoples that received it like a breath of destruction. Whether one looks at the *ergastulas* of ancient Italy, the villages of Russia, the plantations of the southern states or the sugar mills and fazendas of Brazil, it is always ruin, intoxication and death.

(Joaquim Nabuco, *O Abolicionismo*)

CONTENTS

PREFACE

It is my pleasure to thank all those who have helped me in the writing of this book. First, I would like to thank the many people who introduced me to Brazil, its history and culture and the delights of the Portuguese language. I want particularly to thank the staff of the archive of the *Museu Imperial de Petrópolis* for all their help with Princess Isabel's papers. In Russia, as always, the staff of the Russian State Library in Moscow did all they could to help. I am grateful to the British Academy for financial support at the early stage of this project. The Department of History at York has provided a stimulating and friendly environment for research and teaching, both colleagues and students. In particular, I would like to thank Professor James Walvin for his encouragement and Professor Simon Ditchfield for reading the manuscript and making many helpful suggestions. I want to thank students, who for many years have made working in a university such a privilege, especially all the brilliant young women (and the very few young men!) who have taken my course on Catherine the Great over the past three years. My debt to my close friends in Moscow is enormous and has accumulated over twenty years. I would also like to thank Nina Pogosian, Viktoria Loktionova and Alyona Bulakh. Amina, Molly and Finn have been constant in their support and I am forever grateful to them. Two terrible wars feature in this book and, as I write these words, a third one is raging. This book is dedicated to two Ukrainian women, Kateryna Minakova and Olena Ionkina, who embody the spirit of their people and with whom I am privileged to be friends.

Easter 2023, York.

INTRODUCTION

Late in the evening on 13 May 1888 in the city of Petropolis, located high in the *Serra dos Orgaõs* mountain range about 70 km from Rio de Janeiro, an exhausted but jubilant Princess Isabel lay on her bed and wrote a letter to her father, Emperor Dom Pedro II (1831–1889), describing the momentous events of the day.

> My beloved and good Parents
> Not knowing with what to start today, Mummy for having suffered so much these days or Daddy for the day that it is, I am writing to you both jointly. It is from my bed that I am doing this, feeling the need to stretch out after many short nights, long days and commotions of all sorts.
>
> Also it was with a lighter heart that at close to one o'clock we left for Rio with the aim of signing the great law whose great glory belongs to Daddy who for so many years struggled for this end. I also did something for it and I confess that I am very happy for having worked for such a humanitarian and grandiose idea. The manner in which it was passed honours our country and gives me such great joy. The two copies of the law and the decree were signed at 3.30 …[1]

The 'great law' Princess Isabel had signed earlier in the day was known as the *Lei Aurea*, the Golden Law, which abolished slavery immediately and permanently in Brazil. Cheering crowds had met Isabel in Rio de Janeiro, lining the route from the station to the Imperial Palace, showering her with flowers. The palace itself was a sea of humanity in festive mood, waiting for the decisive moment. When Isabel signed the law the crowds went wild. Shouts of '*a Redentora*', the Redeemer, the title by which Isabel was already known, filled the air.[2] At 4.30, Princess Isabel and her family left for Petropolis where

1 Arquivo Grão Para *XLI 3-33 Carta da Princesa Isabel a D. Pedro II 13 de mai 1888.*

2 *Revista Illustrada* 2 June 1888.

Crowds Cheering Princess Isabel just after the signing of the Golden Law
Luiz Ferreira 1888
Public Domain Wikimedia Commons

once again large crowds gathered to greet her. More flowers rained down on Isabel as she attempted to leave the railway station in Petropolis, but the crowd prevented her, wanting to unhitch the horses from Isabel's carriage and pull it from the station to the summer palace. Characteristically, Isabel refused and got out and walked with the crowd.[3] In such a manner, slavery, which more than anything else had defined Brazil as a colony and an independent state, came to an end.

Almost thirty years earlier on 19 February 1861 similar, if more muted, celebrations took place in Russia to mark the abolition of serfdom. Grand Duke Konstantin Nikolaevich, younger brother of Emperor Alexander II (1855–1881), wrote in his diary of the scene that greeted the emperor when he emerged from the Winter Palace.

> Sasha [Alexander] gathered around himself on the manezh all the officers and said to them that today he had declared freedom, that he does not forget that the nobility themselves had renounced serfdom.

3 Arquivo Grão Para *XLI 3-33 Carta da Princesa Isabel a D. Pedro II 13 de mai 1888.*

> And he thanks them as nobles for this and heavily relies on them both as nobles and as officers of his faithful and glorious guard with whom were linked the best memories of his life. The answer to this was such a loud and unanimous 'hurrah' that my heart trembled and tears welled up. This 'hurrah' accompanied Sasha on to the very street itself where the people took it up. It was a marvel. Invasion at Elena Pavlovna's, lunch at Sasha's, evening home. May God bless the new existence of Russia, beginning this very day.[4]

Among those celebrating that day was Grand Duchess Elena Pavlova, the aunt of Alexander and Konstantin. Only the enigmatic hint 'Invasion at Elena Pavlovna's', which was the Grand Duke's shorthand for a gathering at her home, suggested any connection of Elena to the great events of the day. In reality, she had worked tirelessly over the previous six years for the emancipation of the serfs. Unlike Isabel who as regent acted in the full glare of publicity, Elena moved in the numinous, opaque spaces around the person of the emperor where the private and the public and the personal and the political meshed.

Thanksgiving Mass to mark the end of slavery in Brazil 17 May 1888
Antônio Luiz Ferrrira
Public Domain Wikimedia Commons

4 C.V. Mironenko (ed), *Dnevniki Velikogo Kniazhia Konstantina Nikolaevicha. 1858–1864* (Moscow, 2019), p. 272.

Separated by time and space, these two royal women used the opportunities open to them to materially shape the emancipation of serfs and slaves in the empires of Russia and Brazil. In the process, Grand Duchess Elena Pavlovna and Princess Isabel successfully defied the conventions, universal in the nineteenth century, that excluded women from political power. That they both chose to act on the emancipation of serfs and slaves was not a coincidence. In the persons of Elena and Isabel royal power, gender roles and the liberation of servile labour met and had a transformative effect on the outcome of emancipation.

Grand Duchess Elena Pavlovna and Princess Isabel

Grand Duchess Elena Pavlovna of Russia and Princess Isabel of Brazil were principles in the greatest moral drama of the nineteenth century: the emancipation of servile labour. Neither woman is particularly well known. Grand Duchess Elena Pavlovna is barely remembered even by specialists in Russian history and her name has virtually no resonance inside or outside of Russia. Princess Isabel has fared slightly better. She is well known in Brazil, the subject of scholarly and popular biographies and a lively debate on her role in the emancipation of the slaves. However, outside the lusophone world, she is largely unknown.

These two royal women are the subjects of this book. It is not a conventional biography of either of them, but rather a study of three interwoven themes: royalty, gender and emancipation. I am using their lives and political activity to examine the emancipation of serfs in Russia in 1861 and slaves in Brazil in 1888 for the light it casts upon the emancipation process to which both women made a substantial contribution, a contribution that has been undeservedly forgotten. But the study of them illuminates more than two personal stories. Both women were raised in societies with rigid ideas about female roles, servile labour and politics. These two women successfully negotiated the powerful taboos restricting women in all three areas. Showing how they did so reveals both the constraints on them and how these constraints could be bent or even openly defied. Of course, these were not ordinary women, but princesses in monarchical systems in which the ruler was an autocrat in the Russian case and a constitutional monarch, but with real political power, in the Brazilian case. As women, they were excluded from any political role, but as princesses, they were positioned close to the apex of power in both empires. Elena was the sister-in-law of Emperor Nicholas I (1825–1855) and the aunt of Alexander II, while Isabel was the daughter of Emperor Dom Pedro II and the heir to the throne. This closeness to the source of power opened for them opportunities denied to all other women. Even so, neither woman sought to use power or interfere in political matters before the issue of emancipation moved from a forbidden subject into the open and became a live political issue. Only then did Elena and Isabel in their different ways use power in an attempt to bring about the emancipation they desired. The story of how and with what results these royal women became involved in the emancipation of serfs in Russia and slaves in Brazil is the subject matter of this book.

The Empires of Russia and Brazil

Why Russia and Brazil? These are not obvious subjects for comparison. Separated by vast landmasses and oceans, located in different hemispheres, one with a harsh continental climate and the other with a tropical one, the physical differences alone are profound. Culturally, the core of the Russian Empire was Slavic, Orthodox and deeply influenced by its Asiatic heritage. Brazil was lusophone, Catholic and no less influenced by its African heritage. Russia was an autocratic monarchy and Brazil was a constitutional one. The Russian Empire was at the centre of the global great power system while Brazil was on its periphery, barely figuring in the calculations of the great powers. Geography, climate and history placed the two empires on profoundly different trajectories.

Notwithstanding, there is much that makes these two suitable for comparison. Both were vast territories, dwarfing their immediate and distant neighbours. Both were monarchies ruled by European dynasties, the Romanovs and Braganças in Russia and Brazil respectively, sharing the values and traditions of European royalty. The ruling elites in both empires considered themselves European and culturally part of the European world, although this feeling was only partly reciprocated at best by European nations. Located physically and metaphorically on the edges of the European world, their status as Europeans appeared at times decidedly uncertain. The Russian philosopher Nikolai Berdayev described Russia as 'a Christianized Tatar Empire' emphasizing its Asiatic roots.[5] In Brazil, the sheer visibility of its African heritage in Salvador da Bahia or Rio de Janeiro frequently caused foreign visitors to think they were in an African country. John Luccock wrote in the early part of the nineteenth century that a traveller in Rio de Janeiro 'could also believe himself transported to the heart of Africa.'[6] This uncomfortable dissonance between what they desired to be and what they feared they were in actual fact was something that troubled deeply the ruling elites and educated classes in both empires.

---

5 N. Berdayev, *The Origins of Russian Communism* (Michigan, 1970), p. 7.

6 Luiz Carlos Soares, *O 'Povo de Cam' na Capital do Brasil: A Escravidão Urbana no Rio de Janeiro de Século XIX* (Rio de Janeiro, 2007), p. 85.

The empires of Russia and Brazil had more in common as political entities than might seem obvious at first sight. In both empires, the emperors ruled as well as reigned. The social base of both monarchies was the master class which dominated the political systems. In the Russian Empire, the nobility monopolized leading positions in the court, the bureaucracy and the army. In the localities, the nobility was the state. The local administration was controlled by them and they enjoyed untrammelled authority over their estates and those living on them.[7] In the Brazilian Empire, slaveowners and their clients exercised an iron control over the political system at both the national and local levels. They constructed a network of clients which extended deep into urban areas, ensuring that those clients too acted in the interests of the slave-owning elites. Provincial elites cooperated with the national elite in Rio de Janeiro, bound by their shared interest in preserving slavery.[8] In both systems, the owners of servile labour ensured that their interests were not just protected, but were placed beyond discussion: this at a time when the anti-slavery movements in Britain and the United States were mobilizing people on an unprecedented scale. In the Russian Empire, serfdom as an institution was discussed only at the very highest levels of government and under the strictest secrecy. When Nicholas I raised the issue of reform with his most trusted minister, Count Kiselev, the two were alone in Nicholas's study, but even so Nicholas felt obliged to warn Kiselev of the 'necessity to keep his [Nicholas] intentions in strict secrecy.'[9] In the freer Brazilian Empire, the National Assembly observed a convention in which slavery and all matters relating to it were not raised; the press likewise observed a noticeable silence on the issue of slavery.[10]

The monarchy was the capstone of this edifice of power and domination, its own survival tied closely to the interests of those elites. In Russia, Peter III (1762–1762) and Paul I (1796–1801) were murdered by the nobility in the form of the Guards Regiments for egregiously offending them. It was crude, but effective. In Brazil, a more open political system allowed for less drastic methods. Dom Pedro I (1822–1831) was removed from power in 1831 when he sought to free himself from the control of the assembly and constitution, and through this from the dependence on the ruling elites.[11]

7 N.A. Ivanova and V.P. Zheltova, *Soslovnoe Obshchestvo Rossiiskoi Imperii* (Moscow, 2019), pp. 108–109.

8 M. Dolhnikoff, *O Pacto Imperial: Origens do Federalismo no Brasil* (São Paulo, 2005), p. 14.

9 A.P. Zablotskii, *Graf P.D. Kiselev e ero Vremia: Materialy dlia Istorii Imperatorov Aleksandra I, Nikolaia I i Aleksandra II* (4 vols, St. Petersburg, 1882), vol. 2, p. 209.

10 T. Parron, *A Politica da Escravidão no Império do Brasil 1826–186* (Rio de Janeiro, 2011), p. 287.

11 I. Lustosa, *Dom Pedro I* (São Paulo, 2006), pp. 293–295.

Effectively, the ruling elites of both empires appeared to have successfully eliminated all potential threats to their interests from the political systems.

However, the monarchy remained a potential source of weakness in this otherwise closed circle. The monarchy in both empires possessed real power, theoretically enabling it as an institution to move against the interests of the ruling elites under certain circumstances. Even if at the beginning of the nineteenth century few could foresee the circumstances which would allow the monarch to do this, the power of the monarch paradoxically remained the single greatest guarantee of the existing order, but also potentially the greatest threat.

Autocratic power in Russia was real and gave the monarch some autonomy in its relationship with the noble class. From the time of Catherine the Great (1762–1796), all monarchs had trod warily around the issue of serfdom, even though they recognized the harm it brought to the empire. On the other hand, if an emperor was really determined to do something about serfdom, the elites were confronted with a stark choice of accepting it or violently removing the monarch. This had worked effectively in the eighteenth century, but whether it would continue to do so in the nineteenth was a moot question. In Brazil, both Dom Pedro I and his son Dom Pedro II acknowledged the political realities of the power of the slave owners, but both were opposed to slavery. Dom Pedro, I said, 'I know that my blood is of the same colour as that of the negroes.'[12] His son and heir Dom Pedro II described it as 'a terrible curse on the nation'.[13] Ending or restricting servile labour in Russia and Brazil, however, required both changing circumstances and a colossal act of political will at the highest level of the state. What had only been a theoretical possibility became real in 1856 when Alexander II spoke openly to the Moscow nobility about the inevitability of emancipation and in 1867 when Dom Pedro II also spoke about the necessity of emancipation in a speech from the throne at the state opening of Parliament. In both empires, these speeches opened the road, long and winding as it turned out, to emancipation.

Servile Labour

If there were some convergences in the political systems of the two empires, it was in the institution of servile labour that both were most similar. The empires of Russia and Brazil were fully servile societies as distinct from societies in which slaves and serfs existed. Servile societies were much

---

12 Lustosa, *Dom Pedro I,* p. 129.

13 J. Murilo de Carvalho, *Dom Pedro II* (São Paulo, 2007), p. 134.

rarer and what distinguished them from societies with slaves or serfs was that the relationship between the servile class and their owners established the model for all other relationships in their respective societies: political, economic, social and even personal. The unlimited power of one human being over another, its arbitrary application and the use of violence, physical and psychological, to sustain this unequal system of relationships were the defining characteristics of a servile society. A recent magisterial history of Brazil noted that

> [...] slavery was more than an economic system: it moulded conduct, defined social inequalities, made race and colour marks of fundamental difference, mandated behaviour demanding obedience and created a society conditioned by paternalism and strict hierarchy.[14]

That basic relationship rippled through the society, replicating itself in the relationships between an official and subordinate, employer and worker, husband and wife, parents and children. The crude brutality of the master/bondsman relationship was masked in other relationships, but not fundamentally changed.

The empires of Russia and Brazil were two of the few polities that were servile societies from their cores to their peripheries. Republican and Imperial Rome were servile societies as were the British and French West Indies and the southern states of the United States. Neither Britain nor France, however, were servile societies even though they benefitted enormously from their slave colonies. For them, slavery existed overseas in the colonies of the West Indies and had a muted, but very real, presence in the metropolitan areas.[15] In the United States in the nineteenth century, slavery had become ever more a regional phenomenon concentrated in the southern states, even if its pernicious influence continued to seep into the northern states.[16] Countervailing and antagonistic models to servile labour existed in all these countries and in none of them did it provide the only model for political, economic and social relationships. In Russia and Brazil, the institution of servile labour determined all other relationships from the most abstractly political to the most personally intimate. Unravelling those connections was a monumental task.

---

14 L. Schwarcz and H.M. Starling, *Brasil: Uma Biografia* (São Paulo, 2015), p. 96.

15 M. Taylor, *The Interest: How the British Establishment Resisted the Abolition of Slavery* (London, 2020), p. 308.

16 D.B. Davis, *Inhuman Bondage: The Rise and Fall of Slavery in the New World* (Oxford, 2006), p. 280.

The ending of servile labour in all countries was both a national and international affair.[17] That international dimension also played its part in ending serfdom and slavery in Russia and Brazil. Emancipation in Europe, South America and the United States was intimately connected to war and the connection of war and emancipation was apparent in the Russian and Brazilian cases. The interdiction of the slave trade by the British brought Britain and Brazil to the brink of war in the late 1840s, forcing Brazil to finally end the trade in 1851.[18] The Crimean War (1853–1856) and the Paraguayan War (1864–1870) shifted the balance of forces against servile labour in ways that no one had foreseen when the wars began. It was not only hard power that impacted systems of servile labour. By mid-century international public opinion had moved decisively against servile labour and those states that tolerated it. Moral outrage, along with less elevated motives, drove the international campaigns against servile labour. International pariah status was something that deeply troubled the political elites in both empires.

Monarchy and servile labour are two of the three themes of this book. The third is gender. The tens of thousands of women who mobilized against slavery in Europe and the United States emphasized the gendered dimension of the struggle for emancipation, particularly the moral revulsion produced by slavery.[19] Moral outrage can be a potent political force. James Scott, analysing peasant revolt in Southeast Asia, stressed this moral dimension: 'Only the moral vision of these classes and the moral indignation it fosters can begin to explain why peasants may embark on revolt despite seemingly hopeless odds.'[20] It is not stretching the analogy too far to see this moral imperative at work among women, who became the backbone of the anti-slavery movement. This moral indignation inspired multitudes of women to embrace the struggle for emancipation, including the two women who are the focus of the book: Elena and Isabel. As we shall see, political calculations were evident in the actions of both women, but moral outrage was at the heart of their participation to free the serfs and slaves. In this, they differed little from the myriad of other women who participated in the anti-slavery struggle. Morality and politics intersected for these two women as with the anonymous legions who campaigned for freedom elsewhere. The difference was that for Elena and Isabel, the intersection came at the highest level of the state.

---

17 S. Drescher, *Abolition: A History of Slavery and Antislavery* (Cambridge, 2009), p. 267.

18 R. Conrad, *The Destruction of Brazilian Slavery* (Berkeley, 1972), p. 23.

19 J.R. Jeffrey, *The Great Silent Army of Abolitionism: Ordinary Women in the Anti-Slavery Movement* (Chapel Hill, 1998), pp. 36–39.

20 J.C. Scott, *The Moral Economy of the Peasant: Rebellion and Subsistence in Southeast Asia* (New Haven, 1976), p. 192.

For it is another contention of this book that the political struggle to emancipate serfs and slaves at the summit of the state was an essential element of emancipation, not simply the rubber-stamping of a process whose outcome had been predetermined by social and economic forces. For Elena and Isabel, there was nothing inevitable about either the abolition or the terms under which it took place. Other outcomes were possible and indeed more probable than the ones that did occur. Sidney Chalhoub rightly stressed the uncertainty and contingency of events for those participating in them.

> I prefer, therefore, to speak of a 'historical process' not of a transition, the point of the endeavour here is, at least in part, to recover the inconclusiveness, the unpredictability of events, an endeavour that is essential if we want to understand adequately the meaning that historical actors from another epoch attributed to their own struggles.[21]

That political battle over the issue of the emancipation of servile labour opened the way for both Elena and Isabel to abandon traditional gender roles and enter into the public sphere of politics.

Historiography

The historiography of slavery and serfdom has grown exponentially over the last decades, which has enriched our understanding of both systems. There is no space here for a discussion of that literature so I will focus instead on what relates specifically to this book, particularly those works that are comparative in approach and those that focus on Elena or Isabel. The multi-volume *Cambridge History of World Slavery* reflects the prodigious amount of work that has been done on slavery, covering the periods from classical times down to the present. Volume 4 is particularly relevant for this book.[22] Comparative histories of slavery and emancipation are well served by the magisterial works of David Brion Davies and Seymour Drescher.[23] Direct comparisons of the two systems are rare, but there are some important studies.[24] American slavery and Russian serfdom have been admirably compared in Stephen Kolchin's seminal work.[25]

21 S. Chalhoub, *Visões da Liberdade: Uma História das Últimas Décadas da Escravidão na Corte* (São Paulo, 1990), p. 20.

22 D. Eltis, S. Engerman, S. Drescher, D. Richardson (eds), *The Cambridge World History of Slavery: Volume 4, AD 1804–AD 2016* (Cambridge, 2017).

23 Davis, *Inhuman Bondage*; Drescher, *Abolition.*

24 See, for example, M.L. Bush, *Serfdom and Slavery: Studies in Legal Bondage* (London, 2015).

25 S. Kolchin, *Unfree Labour: American Slavery and Russian Serfdom* (Boston, 1990).

But the history of the Americas is not coterminous with the history of the United States. To my knowledge there is nothing comparing Brazilian slavery and Russian serfdom. In Portuguese and in Russian there is an extensive literature on servile labour, but the reluctance of the anglophone world to learn foreign languages means little of it is accessible in English.

The historiography of both Elena and Isabel has struggled to come to terms with these two women and their political roles. The republican regime that replaced the monarchy in 1889 in Brazil lacked both public support and legitimacy and struggled to deal with the overwhelming popularity of '*a Redentora*', as Isabel was widely known, particularly among the poor. It aggressively wrote Isabel out of the emancipation story, replacing her with a series of its own myths that conspicuously failed to catch the popular imagination.[26] Elena fared even worse. The Bolshevik regime combined a theory of history and a visceral hatred of the tsarist regime that effectively silenced any independent research on the role of monarchy in the Soviet Union. More subtly, the Republic in Brazil and the Soviet regime had a profoundly masculine ethos that made them both hostile and blind to the activities of women in politics, particularly royal women.[27] Historiographical fashions in the twentieth century regarding slavery and emancipation concentrated on long-term shifts in the economy from feudalism to capitalism to explain the emancipation of servile labour or stressed the role of the oppressed in bringing about their own emancipation.[28] High politics has been given surprisingly little attention in most accounts of emancipation, seeing the signing of legislation largely as the symbolic ending to a process whose success had been determined elsewhere. This has also deepened the obscurity surrounding the two women since it was in this sphere that they operated. Yet as we shall see, high politics was as crucial to emancipation as shifts in the mode of production or the resistance of the serfs and slaves. Historians have struggled to overcome these legacies to understand the role of women in politics, particularly royal women. Even as women became a legitimate subject for study, royal women in both Brazil and Russia have attracted little attention and accounts of them tend to be dismissed as sycophantic or not serious.[29]

---

26 R. Daibert, *Isabel: A Redentora dos Escravos* (Sao Paulo, 2004), pp. 197–200.

27 B.E. Evans, *Bolshevik Women* (Cambridge, 1997), pp. 58–65. Daibert, *Isabel*, pp. 199–200.

28 See, for example, Emelia Viotti da Costa, *The Brazilian Empire: Myths and Histories* (Chapel Hill, 2000) (revised ed), pp. 170–171.

29 C. Cowling, *Conceiving Freedom: Women of Color, Gender and the Abolition of Slavery in Havana and Rio de Janeiro* (Chapel Hill), pp. 3–4.

Pre-revolutionary historiography in Russia paid little attention to Elena, but the few historians who wrote about her perceived more clearly the political culture in which she operated, above all in the importance that they attributed to personal relationships as a political factor of the utmost importance in Imperial Russia. S.V. Bakhrushin, in a collection of essays commemorating the fiftieth anniversary of emancipation, grasped Elena's mastery of this form of politics.

> Her activity could not be expressed in the direct participation of the working out of this question; her position as a woman and a grand duchess prevented this. She was forced to confine herself to the sphere of those elusive private influences and relations which are not the subject to exact definition, but are often the most decisive.[30]

Soviet historians, not surprisingly had very little to say about Elena, seeing little room for individuals (outside their own pantheon) in epoch-making events such as the emancipation of the serfs and none at all for women and grand duchesses.[31] The exception to this rule was the work of Larissa Zakharova who, alone among Soviet historians, attributed significance to Elena, noting that 'she had a material impact on the reform.'[32] After the stagnation of the Soviet period, the quantity of stimulating and exciting work being produced in Russia is astonishing. Biographies of emperors and empresses, institutional studies, daily routines of the royal family, specific areas of domestic and foreign policy are all the subject of study. In addition, letters, diaries and work journals of various members of the royal family have been published in scholarly editions. As far as Elena is concerned the most important work is a collection of essays, chronicling the breadth of her activity politically, culturally and socially.[33]

Scholars in the West, led by W. Bruce Lincoln, have concentrated on Elena's role in providing a pilot project for the emancipation on her

30 S.V. Bakhrushin, 'Velikaia Kniaginia Elena Pavlovna', in *Osvobozhdenie Krest'ian: Deiateli Reformy* (Moscow, 1911) p. 15. See also A.F. Koni, 'Velikaia Kniaginia Elena Pavlovna' in S.A. Vengerov, *Glavnye Deiateli Osvobozhdeniia Krest'ian* (St. Petersburg, 1903), p. 14.

31 See, for example, P.A. Zaionchkovskii, *Otmena Krepostnogo Prava v Rossii* (Moscow, 1968), pp. 3–6; M.M. Shevchenko, *Istoriia Krepostnogo Prava v Rossii* (Voronezh, 1981), pp.175–176. A more nuanced account can be found in N.M. Druzhinin, *Russkaia Derevnia na Perelome 1861–1880* gg. (Moscow, 1978), pp. 11–18.

32 L.G. Zhakarova, *Samoderzhavie i Otmena Krepostnogo Prava v Rossii 1856–1861* (Moscow, 1984), p. 48.

33 N.A. Beliakov (ed) *Velikaia Kniaginia Elena Pavlovna* (St. Petersburg, 2011).

Karlovka estates in Poltava province, now a part of Ukraine, and in bringing together enlightened bureaucrats, moderate members of the intelligentsia and the emperor.[34] Elena provided the introductions and then, as demanded by the prevailing ideology, slipped discreetly into the background, allowing the men to get on with the great business of emancipation. Only Alfred J. Rieber recognized that Elena was not simply an accomplished salonniere, but a key player in the ongoing struggle for an emancipation, and a radical one to boot.[35] Elena, however, was not the main focus of Rieber's account and her importance to emancipation and both the mode of her political activity and its results still remain to be fully clarified. A recent study of Elena gives a detailed account of her life at the Russian court, describing her life and her many achievements. But on the matter of the great battle for emancipation, it rather downplays Elena's role.[36]

In contrast to Elena, Isabel has been the subject of several studies, scholarly and popular, which examine her private life and her actions as regent, particularly those that related to abolition. A recent popular biography of Isabel emphasized her lack of any serious interest in politics, her activity being guided far more by her Catholicism and traditional notions of charity than political conviction.[37] An important and groundbreaking study acknowledges Isabel as a political actor, but stresses her conservatism.[38] Even a very impressive scholarly biography of Isabel emphasizes her lack of interest in politics, her one assertion of power in 1888 costing her the throne.[39] The latter biography, while rightly stressing Isabel's experience as a woman in a patriarchal society, does not give sufficient attention to Isabel as empress-in-waiting, not just in name, but in her growing sense of power and authority. Only one study of emancipation grasps the importance of Isabel as a political actor in the final year of slavery's existence, acknowledging her skill as a politician and how radical her actions were.[40] Despite the recent

34 W. Bruce Lincoln, 'The Karlovka Reform', *Slavic Review*, 28 (1969) pp. 463–471; Lincoln, 'The Circle of Grand Duchess Elena Pavlovna, 1848–1861', *Slavonic and East European Review*, 48 (1970), pp. 373–387; Lincoln, *In the Vanguard of Reform: Russia's Enlightened Bureaucrats, 1825–1861* (Dekalb, IL, 1982), pp. 148–162. This view of Elena can also be seen in D. Moon, *The Abolition of Serfdom in Russia, 1762–1907* (Harlow, 2001), p. 127.

35 A. Rieber, *The Politics of the Autocracy: Letters of Alexander II to Prince A.I. Bariatinskii* (The Hague, 1966), p. 49.

36 M. Soroka and Charles Ruud, *Becoming a Romanov: Grand Duchess Elena of Russia and Her World* (1807–1873) (Farnham, 2015).

37 M.del Priore, *O Castelo de Papel* (Rio de Janeiro, 2013), p. 218.

38 Daibert, *Isabel*, p. 110.

39 R.J. Barman, *Princess Isabel of Brazil: Gender and Power in the Nineteenth Century* (Willington, 2002), p. 249.

40 E. Silva, *As Camélias do Leblon e a Abolição da Escravatura* (São Paulo, 2003), p. 37.

outpouring of scholarship on Isabel, the criticisms raised by Maria de Lourdes Viana Lyra in 1998 are still valid: 'Her image appears always and only linked with the final movement on behalf of the abolition of slavery and most often linked only to the signing of the so-called "Golden Law."'[41] Isabel emerges from most of these accounts as a deeply religious, apolitical woman finally galvanized into action by the anti-slavery movement crashing over the country in the 1880s. Her decisions are depicted as spontaneous, inspired by her Catholicism and without much foresight of the consequences. These portraits fit rather closely with women as passive, lacking strong political convictions and dependent, which was the model of Isabel's own time. Isabel was none of these things. By the time of her third regency in 1887–1888 she was an experienced, determined politician with strong convictions and the strength of character and political nous to enforce her will.

The accounts of Elena and Isabel that, in my opinion, capture best the two women as political actors are unpublished dissertations from the universities of Moscow in Russia and Severino Sombra in Brazil. Ekaterina Reznikova argued that 'the personality and actively of Grand Duchess Elena Pavlovna was a significant, and in some cases decisive, influence on the development and ratification of the model of reform in 1861.'[42] Maria de Luiza de Carvalho sought 'to construct a new image of Isabel, privileging her position as a political actor that shows that she was not a revolutionary, nor just the "Redentora" but a woman of her time, divided between her strong religiosity and notions of progress and modernity'.[43] It is this understanding of Elena and Isabel that I share.

Sources

This book is based primarily on Russian and Brazilian sources, both archival and published. Regarding Elena Pavlovna I have used overwhelmingly the diaries, memoirs, letters and reminiscences of those who knew her, particularly those who worked with her in the momentous years 1855–1861. As a woman, she did not participate in state bodies, nor engage in official correspondence with them. This is what has made it so challenging to reconstruct how she accessed and used

41 M de Lourdes Viana Lyra 'Isabel de Brangança, Uma Princesa Imperial', *Revista do Instituto Histórico e Geográfico Brasileiro*, 158 (1997), p. 83.

42 E.E. Reznikova, *Velikaia Kniaginia Elena Pavlovna v Politicheskoi i Kul'turnoi Zhizni Rossii: 1824–173 gg.* (Unpublished dissertation, Moscow, 1998), p. 261. (Part of Reznikova's work has been published in Beliakov, *Velikaia Kniaginia Elena Pavovna.*)

43 M. Luiza de Carvalho Mesquita, *O 'Terceiro Reinado': Isabel de Bragança, A Imperatriz Que Não Foi* (Unpublished dissertation, Vassouras, 2009), p. 177.

power. But it also provided an opportunity to look at the informal side of politics in Tsarist Russia, those 'elusive personal relations' referred to by Bakhrushin. These 'personal sources' open up a world in which speech, tone of voice, gesture and physical proximity to the person of the emperor take on real significance and have real consequences in the intense competition for power and influence on the emperor. This type of power, particularly when wielded by a woman, depended on subtlety, discretion and self-effacement, which adds to the challenge of identifying it. However, it is possible to reconstruct it, at least in outline.

For Isabel, I have used contemporary newspapers and journals, published documents, and memoirs. The most important source, however, has been the letters that Isabel wrote to her father during her regencies, particularly her third regency when the emancipation took place. The letters can be at times rather cloying. Isabel even as a grown woman frequently began her letters with various endearments such as '"my beloved little daddy" and ended with "your little daughter and little chatterbox friend"'[44] Nevertheless, beyond the opening and closing formalities, the letters are unmatched as a source for understanding Isabel's actions in her own words to the man she was closest to for most of her life. In addition to the letters, I have used what has been called her 'testament'.[45] This was a document handwritten by Isabel in December 1888 for her children in which she explicitly explained the motivations for her actions that led, as she saw it, to the signing of the Golden Law in May of that year. The testimony was written on notepaper, never revised and abandoned when Isabel and her family went into exile the following year.

44 See, for example, *Arquivo Grão Pará* XLI.3.16 *Carta da Princesa Isabel a D. Pedro II 18 January 1871.*

45 *Acervo do Arquivo Historico do Museu Imperial Maco* 1999 – Doc 9030.

Chapter 1

EMPIRES OF SERVILITY

Slavery is a cancer rotting Brazil

–Emperor Dom Pedro 1[1]

The serf system is a powder keg under the state…

–Count Beckendorf to Nicholas I 1839[2]

For centuries, servile labour exercised a determining influence on the political, economic and social life of the Russian Empire and Brazil both as a Portuguese colony and as the Empire of Brazil from 1822. Beginning as a system of coerced labour, it had metastasized into all parts of the body politic of both empires, leaving no area of life free from its taint. The institutions and values of the two empires were so thoroughly permeated by the existence of servile labour that its abolition appeared unthinkable, let alone practicable. Yet the pressure for abolition rose inexorably in the nineteenth century, making the inconceivable conceivable and the unachievable achievable.

The Russian and Brazilian empires were not immune to the demand for abolition that swept Europe and the Americas, but they were able to resist it until the second half of the nineteenth century. The institution of servile labour, central to all aspects of life in both empires, was fiercely defended by the master class, who resisted each and every attempt, however modest, to limit its power over serfs or slaves. The tenacious defence of slavery and serfdom by the serf and slave owners made abolition an existential matter for both empires, calling into question the constitutional, economic and social structures. If this was not enough, the abolition of serfdom and slavery marked only the start of a fundamental transformative process whose end could not be foreseen. What was to happen to the freed bondsman? How were they to be integrated into their respective societies? How was the relationship between

1 Lustosa, *Dom Pedro I*, p. 129.

2 B.A. Fedorov (ed), *Konets Krepostnichestva v Rossii: Dokumenty, Pis'ma, Memuary, stat'i* (Moscow, 1994), p. 63.

the ruling class and the state to be reconstructed in the aftermath of such a traumatic breakdown? The answers to these questions tended to be stark and bleak: the destruction of the state, the collapse of the economy, the end of private property: in short, the ruin of civilization. Given such a vista, it is hardly surprising that in neither empire was there much enthusiasm for undertaking such a risky enterprise.

Nevertheless, decisive political action ended serfdom in 1861 in Russia and slavery in 1888 in Brazil, giving individual freedom to the serfs and slaves, overcoming the opposition of the master class and embracing all the consequent risks of emancipation. To understand how this came about, we need to look at the nature of servility in both empires, their monarchical political structure and the unique issue of emancipation as a political and moral necessity.

Serfdom and Slavery

Russian serfdom and Brazilian slavery were not identical. In terms of brutality, degradation and exploitation nothing could match the racial slavery of the New World until the slave labour camps of the Nazi and Communist regimes of the twentieth century. The sugar plantations of Brazil and the Caribbean and the cotton plantations of the Southern United States plumbed new depths of cruelty, greed and dehumanization. Not surprisingly, the racial slavery of the Americas has indelibly shaped the modern understanding of slavery. However, slavery existed, and exists, in many forms. It was present in the first human civilizations in Mesopotamia and has enjoyed an unbroken existence down to our own times. Slaves could be domestic servants, field hands, soldiers, concubines or advisers to emperors. While slaves had in common their absolute dependence on a master, the individual experience of slavery differed greatly. The protean nature of slavery has allowed it to adapt to any economic or political system from the most democratic to the most despotic, from classical Athens to Nazi Germany.[3] Serfdom, a lesser form of bonded labour, was much more common in Europe than slavery and was distinguished from slavery by the legal protections the serf enjoyed and the fact that the serf was normally a member of the wider community.[4] Nevertheless, serfs, like slaves, deeply resented their servile status and serf revolts were a sporadic, but endemic feature of European history. Like slavery, however, serfdom varied in its levels of oppression and exploitation. As we shall, Russian serfdom was much closer to slavery than to the serfdoms of Central and Western Europe.

3 Davis, *Inhuman Bondage*, pp. 32–37.
4 Bush, *Servitude in Modern Times*, pp. 20–21.

Russian serfdom and Brazilian slavery were products of the early modern era. In a 200-year period spanning the fifteenth to the seventeenth centuries, Russian serfdom and Brazilian slavery took on their distinctive forms. Over the centuries millions lived and died in servitude. At the time of abolition, there were approximately 48 million serfs in Russia: 22.5 million were serfs belonging to nobles, 23.5 million belonged to the state and almost 2 million to the crown. Together they made up 80% of the total population.[5] Between 1550 and 1850, 3.5 million slaves were imported into Brazil, 38% of the total number of slaves taken to the New World.[6] In Brazil, on the eve of emancipation, there were 723,419 slaves, the vast majority concentrated in the coffee-producing provinces of São Paulo, Rio de Janeiro and Minas Gerais.[7] The percentage of slaves expressed as a part of the total population had declined substantially over the nineteenth century. In 1817/18, they made up 50% of the population, and by 1874 that had fallen to just under 16%.[8] The numbers themselves were substantial, but the cumulative effect of centuries of bondage conditioned every aspect of life in the two empires, making abolition a herculean task.

Brazilian Slavery

Long before the Portuguese landed in Brazil, they already had extensive experience with African slavery thanks to the Moorish conquest of Portugal. By mid-sixteenth century, 10 per cent of the population of Lisbon were slaves.[9] The real innovation of the Portuguese was to use African slaves for sugar production. The Portuguese had developed the prototypes of plantation slavery in the Atlantic islands of São Tome and Madeira in the fifteenth century using African slave labour.[10] In Salvador de Bahia and Pernambuco in Brazil, the conditions were ideal for the production of sugar on a much greater scale than the Atlantic islands and the Portuguese were quick to exploit the opportunity. By the end of the sixteenth century, 140 sugar plantations or *engenhos* as they were known in Brazil were operating in the Reconcavo area of Bahia.[11] As on the Atlantic islands, African slave labour was the obvious solution to the labour shortage though the demand for slaves was of a completely different magnitude.

---

5 F.W. Wcislo, *Reforming Rural Russia: State, Local Society, and National Politics 1855, 1914* (Princeton, 1990), pp. 7–8.

6 K.M. Mattos, *To Be a Slave in Brazil 1550–1888* (Rutgers, 1986) pp. 40–41.

7 Conrad, *The Destruction of Brazilian Slavery*, p. 285.

8 Conrad, *The Destruction of Brazilian Slavery*, pp. 283–84.

9 Schwarcz, *Brasil Uma Biografia*, p. 80.

10 Klein, *Slavery in Brazil*, pp. 11–12.

11 Schwarcz, *Brasil: Uma Biografia*, p. 52.

The sugar plantations of Brazil originated in mass violence and were maintained by it. African slaves were ripped from their homes, transported in the lethal conditions of the middle passage and disgorged into a world with an alien language, religion and culture, a world in which they were isolated, humiliated and mercilessly exploited. Slaves arriving in Rio de Janeiro were sold in the *Mercado do Valongo* in the very heart of the city and without the least attempt at discretion.[12] Maria Graham, a British traveller in Brazil in the 1820s, saw at first hand the slave market of Valongo in Rio and a similar one in Recife, both closer to a charnel house than a market.

> We had hardly gone fifty paces into Recife, when we were absolutely sickened by the first sight of a slave market. It was the first time either the boys or I had been in a slave-country; and, however strong and poignant the feelings maybe at home, when imagination pictures slavery, they are nothing compared to the staggering sight of a slave market. It was thinly stocked, owing to the circumstances of the town; which cause most of the owners of new slaves to closely shut them up in the depôts. Yet about fifty young creatures, boy and girls, with all the appearance of disease and famine consequent upon scanty food and long confinement in unwholesome places, were sitting and lying among the filthiest animals in the streets. The sight sent us home to the ship with heart-ache and resolution, 'not loud, but deep', that nothing in our power should be considered too little, or too great, that can tend to abolish or to alleviate slavery.[13]

The slave market was only the beginning of a world defined by exploitation, abuse and, for many, an early death. The *engehnos* or sugar plantations of Brazil were the prototypes for all the plantations of the New World, pioneering both the remorseless work regimes and the systems of violence necessary to maintain them. Life expectancy for a slave on a Brazilian plantation was low, approximately five years.[14] For the master, however, five years of work represented a very handsome return, a doubling of his investment in the slave.[15]

---

12 Soares, *O 'Povo de Cam'*, pp. 39–43.

13 J. Hayward and M. Caballero (eds), *Maria Graham's Journal of a Voyage to Brazil* (Anderson, 2010), p. 38.

14 Schwartz, *Sugar Plantations*, p. 106.

15 Schwartz, *Slaves, Peasants and Rebels*, p. 42.

Rua do Valongo (Slave market in Rio de Janeiro)
Jean-Baptiste Debret 1820–1830
Public Domain Wikimedia Commons

Plantation slavery was the archetypal form of slavery in Brazil and the Americas as a whole. Brazilian slavery, however, was remarkably diverse, taking many forms. Muleteers, leading mule trains deep into the interior of the country, were often slaves. In Rio Grande de Sul in the south, on the great cattle ranches, slaves served as cowboys. Slaves dug the gold and diamonds out of the mines of Minas Gerais, delivering unparalleled wealth to Portugal in the eighteenth century.[16] The experience of such slaves was a world away from the intensely supervised life of the sugar, cotton and coffee plantations. While life in the mines, on cattle drives or mule trains was hard and dangerous, it was prized because of the autonomy it gave slaves.[17] These men were still slaves, but for large parts of their lives they were free of direct control.

Brazilian cities teemed with slaves, freedmen and their descendants. Domestic slaves were an integral part of urban and rural life in Brazil, doing the household chores and serving as status symbols for their masters.

16 Klein and Vinson, *African Slavery in Latin America*, p. 72.

17 A.J. Russell-Wood, *Slavery and Freedom in Colonial Brazil* (Oxford, 2002) p. 60.

All the manual labour in Brazilian cities was carried out by slaves as even the Portuguese poor shunned physical work and dreamed of owning slaves.[18] Brazilian slavery was ubiquitous and slaves could be found in all parts of the enormous country, not just in a particular region or on the periphery. Only in the final decades of slavery did it become a regional phenomenon as more and more slaves were sucked into coffee-producing provinces of São Paulo, Rio de Janeiro and Minas Gerais.

Escravidão de ganho or slavery for profit was a peculiarity of Brazilian slavery that sharply distinguished it from the slavery of the United States or the Caribbean and had much in common with the system of *obrok* among Russian serfs. Instead of labouring directly for their masters, *escravos de ganho* were required to deliver a cash sum to their masters at the end of the day, week or month.[19] Slaves, like Russian serfs, had a distinct preference for this type of work because it gave them the chance to earn money beyond what they had to pay to their owners, but above all because it gave them a much higher degree of autonomy and control over their lives. They thronged the streets of Rio de Janeiro and Salvador carrying large burdens, washing clothes at the public fountains and practicing every type of trade. Thomas Ewbank, an American, was struck by this aspect of city life.

> Slaves of both sexes cry wares through every street. Vegetables, flowers, fruits, edible roots, fowls, eggs, and every rural product; cakes pies, rusks, *doces*, confectionary, 'heavenly bacon' etc., pass your windows continually. Your cook wants a skillet, and, hark! The signal of a pedestrian coppersmith is heard; his bell is a stew pan, and the clapper a hammer. A water-pot is shattered; in half and hour a moringue-merchant approaches.[20]

In Rio de Janeiro, the streets were completely dominated by slaves in the mid-day heat.[21] The visibility and the apparently free movement of slaves gave Brazilian cities the pronounced African aspect so often commented on by visitors.[22] Slaves moved around the cities with a freedom and lack of

---

18 J. Reis, *Rebelião Escrava no Brasil: A Historia do Levante dos Malês em 1835* (São Paulo, 2003), p. 31.

19 Soares, *O 'Povo de Cam'*, p. 123.

20 T. Ewbank, *Life in Brazil or a Journal of a Visit to the Land of the Cocoa and the Palm* (New York, 1856), pp. 92–93.

21 S. Barra, *Entre a Corte e a Cidade: O Rio de Janeiro no tempo do Rei (1808–1821)* (Rio de Janeiro, 2008), pp. 218–19.

22 Soares, *O 'Povo de Cam'*, p. 126.

Ceremonial greeting serfs and masters. Print (1904)
Christian Bos

supervision that would have astonished masters and slaves in the United States where slave movement was much more tightly controlled. The large numbers of freedmen in Brazil made it even more difficult to supervise slaves, which proved a constant headache for the police.[23]

Russian Serfdom

Russian serfdom was a form of chattel slavery. If it did not plumb the depths of degradation and exploitation of the racial slavery of the Americas, it was still slavery in all but name. Important differences distinguished Russian serfdom from Brazilian slavery: most notably, Russian serfs were rooted in their communities and shared an ethnic identity with their masters. The sharp, racial cleavage between master and slave and the traumatic experience of the middle passage had no counterpart in Russian serfdom. However, the shared ethnicity of the master and serf was only

23 Barra, *Entre a Corte e a Cidade*, p. 229.

a superficial covering that masked a chasm between the two groups. The cultural reforms of the autocracy begun by Peter the Great had created a Europeanized elite while the serfs remained locked into the pre-Petrine Muscovite culture. These differences manifested themselves in the increasing alienation and mutual incomprehension of the two groups. The division between them had become so great by the end of the eighteenth century that few of the nobility were willing to accept that they shared a common humanity with the serfs. Catherine the Great commented ruefully: 'You hardly dare say that they are just the same people as we; and when I myself say this, I risk having stones hurled at me.'[24] If the cultural difference between a Russian serf and his noble master did not match the racial difference between the Brazilian slave and master, it was nevertheless a chasm that went way beyond class difference.[25] The hatred of the peasantry for the gentry was expressed in the Pugachev rebellion 1773–1775 and indeed outlived serfdom, erupting in both the 1905 and the 1917 revolutions.

Formal slavery had existed in Russia until Peter the Great abolished it in 1723, largely because too many peasants were selling themselves into slavery or claiming slave status to avoid state taxes and conscription.[26] The line between slave and serf, however, remained very blurred. Jerome Blum, the author of the most authoritative book on the Russian peasantry in English, wrote: 'By the last quarter of the eighteenth century the Russian serf was scarcely distinguishable from a chattel slave.'[27] The debased position of the Russian serf in the nineteenth century was ably summarized in recent history.

> Peasants and household servants (*dvorovye liudi*) were the object of this law, part of the immovable property of the noble, which was transferred through inheritance. The noble had the right to sell and buy peasants, offer them as collateral, resettle them on different estates. And although at the beginning of the nineteenth century the sale of serfs in person without land in markets and trades was forbidden and the publication of notice about the sale of serfs in newspapers was no longer allowed, it did not change the essence of the matter.[28]

---

24 J.T. Alexander, *Catherine the Great: Life and Legend* (Oxford, 1989), p. 119.
25 A. Etkind, *Internal Colonization: Russia's Imperial Experience* (Cambridge, 2011), p. 111.
26 R. Hellie, *Slavery in Russia 1450–1725* (Chicago, 1982), pp. 698–703.
27 Blum, *Lord and Peasant in Russia*, p. 422.
28 Ivanova and Zheltova, *Soslovoe Obshchestvo Rossiiskoi Imperii*, p. 500.

Sale of a serf girl
Nikolai Nevrev 1866
Public Domain Wikimedia Commons

The serf owed his master duties either in the form of labour (*barshchina*) or cash (*obrok*) *Barshchina* consisted of direct, supervised labour on the landlord's demesne, while *obrok* was cash payments delivered at specified times and in specified amounts. Russian serfs, like *escravos de ganho* in Brazil, much preferred *obrok* to *barshchina* because it gave them the chance to earn more money for themselves and, above all, because it gave them more autonomy.[29] Recent studies suggest that demands on the serf were growing in the nineteenth century and an increasing number were shifted to *barshchina* as landlords attempted to take advantage of the developing international market in grain. If Russian serfdom did not deliver the spectacular profits of the coffee plantations of Rio de Janeiro or Sao Paulo in the nineteenth century, it continued to generate substantial incomes for the gentry. In no economic sense had it entered a terminal crisis at the time of emancipation.[30]

---

29 Blum, *Lord and Peasant in Russia*, p. 448.

30 Moon, *The Abolition of Serfdom in Russia*, pp. 20–21.

The serf-master had a broad array of judicial powers to enforce his authority over the serf from flogging, conscription into the army or permanent exile with hard labour to Siberia. The serf had no legal avenue of appeal against his master; the last loophole, that of direct appeal to the emperor, was closed off by Catherine the Great in 1765. A serf owner was not allowed to deliberately kill a serf, but as Alexander Radishchev tartly commented 'the law forbids us to take their life, that is to take it suddenly.'[31] Portuguese and Brazilian law explicitly forbade the killing of slaves, lest it be thought this theoretical limitation distinguished the Russian serf from a slave.[32] There were no legal limits to the degree of exploitation of serfs until Emperor Paul restricted the number of days serfs could be forced to work for their master or mistress to three a week, although this seems to have had little effect in reality.[33] The exploitation of serfs did not end with dues to the master or mistress. He was liable for taxes to the state and conscription into the army, which, far from helping integrate the serf into society, was yet another mark of his debased status. No slaves in the Americas suffered these last two impositions.

The power of the master over his serf was limited only by self-restraint, economic self-interest and peer pressure from surrounding nobles. None of these barriers effectively restrained the caprice of the master. In the 1750s, Countess Daria Saltykova unleashed a torrent of the most sadistic violence against her serfs, murdering at least 75, of whom 72 were women. Saltykova beat her house servants with whips, iron bars and sticks.[34]

> She, living in Moscow and in summer on her Moscow estates, was able in the course of six years and with her own hands to beat her women with a cylinder, with canes, with logs, with an iron bar, a whip, a knout. She set fire to the hair on their head, tore their ears with red hot pincers, poured boiling water on their face and beat their head off a wall. In winter, after punishment, she forced men and women to stand barefoot in the frost, tortured them with cold and she got away with it all.[35]

Saltykova was exceptional, but the system was designed to make it almost impossible for serfs to bring a successful complaint against their masters. Most

---

31 Radishchev, *A Journey*, p. 221.

32 Klein and Luna, *Slavery in Brazil*, p. 192.

33 R. McGrew, *Paul I of Russia 1754–1801* (Oxford, 1992) p. 238.

34 G.I. Studenkin, 'Saltychika 1730–1801', *Russkaia Starina*, 10 (1874), pp. 526–28.

35 V. Semevskii, 'Krepostnye Krest'iane pri Ekaterine II' *Russkaia Starina*, 17 (1876), p. 618.

serf owners, even those who regarded themselves as models of enlightenment, saw nothing wrong in routinely flogging serfs for various misdemeanours or out of sheer caprice.[36] Russian memoir literature is full of anecdotes about the violent eccentricities of serf owners. Among others, the writer Ivan Turgenev, the anarchist revolutionary Prince Kropotkin and Petr Semenov Tian-Shankskii, one of the architects of emancipation, all left vivid accounts of the arbitrary violence of their parents towards the serfs.[37] Memoir literature can be dismissed as anecdotal and untypical, but in this respect, there is a near unanimity that makes it hard to dismiss. The very few narratives emanating directly from the serfs themselves also emphasized this power.[38] Serf women, like slave women, were in addition vulnerable to the sexual coercion of their masters or their master's sons. The most damaging aspect of serfdom lay not so much in the spectacular but rare acts of cruelty, such as those carried out by Countess Saltykova, but in the constant and complete dependence on the will of another. Richard Stites' judgement on serfdom emphasized its psychological cruelty.

> But it is not just the number of abused victims or their level of self-indulgence or even the mechanism of their exploitation that marked serfdom as a scourge. It was embedded in the very culture of unfreedom, the dark shadow of uncertainty, whim, or malicious decision by a lord who could alter – and ruin – someone's life. Of all the forms of servitude, domestic serfdom, in the view of the great reformer-in-exile Nikolai Turgenev, was 'the most hideous and repulsive'.[39]

In this, as in much else, Russian serfdom resembled the slavery of the New World.

The parallels between serfdom in its Russian form and slavery were not lost on educated contemporaries. Alexander Radishchev's description of the evils of serfdom in his *Journey From St. Petersburg to Moscow*, published in 1790, was heavily influenced by Abbe Raynal's *History of the Two Indies*, a passionate condemnation of West Indian slavery.[40] Very frequently, those

36 K.P. Antonova, *An Ordinary Marriage: The World of a Gentry Family in Provincial Russia* (Oxford, 2013), p. 65.

37 See, for example, P. Tian-Shanskii, *Memuary* (5 vols, Moscow, 2018) vol. III, p. 55.

38 J. McKay (ed), *Four Russian Serf Narratives* (Madison, WI, 2009).

39 R. Stites, *Serfdom, Society and the Arts in Imperial Russia: The Pleasure and the Power* (Princeton, 2005), pp. 82–83.

40 Radischchev, *A Journey*, pp. 24–25.

writing or discussing serfdom did not bother to distinguish between serfdom and slavery. Instead of using the technical term for serfdom, *krepostnoe pravo* or *krepostnichestvo*, they used the word *rabstvo*, slavery. Before he became emperor, Alexander I wrote in his diary: 'Nothing could be more humiliating and inhuman than the sale of human beings and so it is absolutely necessary to start by promulgating an edict that will forbid it forever. To the shame of Russia, slavery still exists here.'[41] In 1834, Emperor Nicholas I told Count P. D. Kiselev, his most trusted minister, 'Since I came to the throne I have gathered all the documents relating to the procedures which I want to introduce against slavery when the time comes to free the peasants in the entire empire.'[42] It could be argued that it was intellectual laziness that led the Romanov male monarchs, not generally noted for their love of learning, to use slavery rather than serfdom. However, Kiselev himself, the man who knew more about serfdom from a legal and technical point of view than anyone else in the empire in the nineteenth century, prepared a paper for Nicholas I entitled *On the Gradual Abolition of Slavery (rabstvo) in Russia.*[43] Alexander Herzen, one of the towering figures of opposition to Nicholas I and later Alexander II, frequently used the term slavery when writing about serfdom. In an appeal to the Russian nobility in 1853, for example, he wrote

> 'There is no freedom for us while the curse of serfdom hangs over us, while in our midst there continues to exist the vile, shameful, completely unjustified slavery of the peasants.'[44]

This elision of slavery and serfdom in the writings and words of contemporaries reflected the perception that Russian serfdom was a form of slavery. Curiously, this understanding of the essence of Russian serfdom survives to this day. On the statue erected to Alexander II in 2007 on the grounds of the Church of Christ the Saviour in Moscow, one of the country's most sacred spaces, part of the inscription reads: *The Tsar-Liberator … who freed the Russian people from slavery.* Again the word used is slavery (*rabstvo*), not serfdom.

Brazilian slavery and Russian serfdom differed in their origins, the racial distinction between master and bondsman in Brazil, which had no direct equivalent in Russia, and in the sheer number of bondsmen in the Russian Empire compared to Brazil. Despite the manifold differences, there was considerable

41 M.-P. Rey, *Alexander I: The Tsar Who Defeated Napoleon* (Dekalb, Illinois, 2012), p. 77.
42 Zablotskii-Desiatovskii, *Graf P.D. Kiselev*, vol. 2, p. 210.
43 Zablotskii-Desiatovskii, *Graf P.D. Kiselev,* vol. 2, p. 204.
44 K. Parthé (ed), *A Herzen Reader* (Evanston, Illinois, 2012), p. 31.

Stature to the Tsar Liberator 2005
Public Domain

The inscription reads:
Emperor Aleksandr II
abolished serfdom (krepostnoe pravo) in Russia and freed millions of peasants from many centuries of slavery (rabstvo) in 1861.
He introduced military and legal reforms and a system of local self-government with town and zemstvo councils.
He ended the long Caucasian War.
He freed the Slavic peoples from the Ottoman yoke.
He died 1 March 1881 as a result of a terrorist act.

overlap between the two. Slavery and serfdom were ubiquitous in both empires, concentrated in the core areas, but also reaching the peripheries. Russian serfdom became more commercially orientated with the development of the grain trade in the nineteenth century just as Brazilian slaves in some respects were coming to resemble peasants with small plots of land and livestock, even while they remained slaves.[45] Even though the racial difference was not replicated between Russian master and serf, the cultural difference was so profound

45 F. Dos Santos Gomes, *Histórias de Quilombolas: Mocambos e Comunidades de Senzalas no Rio de Janeiro, Século XIX* (São Paulo, 2006), p. 52.

that many Russian nobles did not recognize the basic humanity of their serfs. Above all, however, Russian serfdom and Brazilian slavery resembled each other in the cumulative effect the system of bondage had on their societies. Rather than being societies with slaves or serfs, they were servile societies in the full meaning of this term. It is to this that we now turn.

Servile Societies

The *ergastulas* of Ancient Rome, the plantations in the Southern United States, the villages of Russia and the fazendas of Brazil were, in the eyes of the great Brazilian abolitionist Joaquim Nabucco, united by the 'breath of destruction' that passed over them and their societies. What he was describing, although he did not use the term, were servile societies. The epigraphs at the start of this book suggested that contemporaries in Russia and Brazil recognized that they were kindred systems.

In Russia and Brazil, the father of the family, whether nobleman or peasant, wielded despotic powers over the members of the family.[46] The manifestation of that power was traumatic not only for the serf on the receiving end but for the members of the serf owners family too. Prince Kropotkin, described the atmosphere in the house after his father had imposed a savage flogging on his manservant as 'terror and absolute muteness reign in the house'.[47] Children of the master class, however, had to be trained for their roles as future masters and overcome any squeamishness about the cruelties of the system. Catherine the Great saw with her own eyes how the Russian aristocracy prepared their children for their future roles:

> The inclination to despotism is cultivated better there than in any other inhabited place on the planet. It is instilled in them from early childhood when they see with what cruelty their parents deal with their servants. After all, there isn't a house in which there wouldn't be iron collars, chains and various other tools for the torment for the smallest infringements by those whom nature has placed in this unhappy class.[48]

In Brazil, the British resident Henry Koster described how children of the slaveowners were groomed for their roles.

---

46 V.V. Ponomareva and L.B. Khoroshilova *Mir Russkoi Zhenshchiny: Sem'ia, Professiia, Domashnii Uklad XVIII–Nachalo XX veka* (Moscow, 2016), p. 19. S. Graham, *House and Street: The Domestic World of Servants and Masters in Nineteenth Century Rio de Janeiro* (Cambridge, 1995), pp. 10–11.

47 P. Kropotkin, *Memoirs of a Revolutionist* (New York, 1971,) p. 51.

48 Empress Catherine II, *Zapiski Imperatritsy Ekateriny Velikoi* (St. Petersburg, 1907), pp. 174–75.

> As soon as child begins to crawl, a slave of about its own age and of the same sex is given to it as a playfellow, or rather a plaything; they grow up together, and the slave is made the stock upon which the young owner gives vent to his passion; the slave is sent upon all errands, and the receives the blame for all unfortunate accidents.[49]

In both empires, children of the master class were initiated into their roles as masters very early. A few like Kropotkin or Nabuco rebelled against the whole system. Most simply accepted it and replicated it when they became masters in their turn.

The political systems in both empires complemented the master–slave relationship. In Russia, the autocracy reflected the social system in a very direct way. Serfdom and autocracy existed in harmony with the unlimited and arbitrary power of the serf owner mirroring the unlimited and arbitrary power of the autocracy. In Brazil, liberal democracy at first sight would seem to contain the same contradiction as existed in the United States in which the founding ideals of the state were directly opposed to slavery. That contradiction, however, only becomes politically important if it is pointed out. Unlike in the United States, very few are troubled to do this. In 1823, José Bonifácio de Andrada e Silva, the father of Brazilian independence, addressed precisely this question to the National Assembly: 'But how can there be a stable liberal Constitution in a country continually inhabited by an immense multitude of brutish slaves and enemies.'[50] His, however, was a lone voice and the slave-owning elite for decades effectively shut down any discussion of slavery in Parliament or the press.[51] In these circumstances, liberal democracy proved very hospitable to slavery. The electoral system was dominated by the slaveowners and their clients, ensuring that their interests, above all slavery, were protected. Slaveowners controlled the provincial administration, the system of voting and the two political parties, the Conservatives and Liberals. Whatever differences existed between the parties, for many decades, they were at one when it came to slavery. The parliamentary system would prove the last bastion of slavery and was only broken by the direct intervention of Princess Isabel. There was no Gordian knot to cut in either Russia or Brazil when it came to emancipation. Unravelling an institution integral to every aspect of society was complicated, fraught with risk and deeply unpredictable.

---

49 H. Koster, *Travels in Brazil* (London, 1816), pp. 389–90.

50 J. Caldeira, *José Bonifácio de Andrade e Silva* (São Paulo, 2002), p. 201.

51 Parron, *A Política da Escravidão,* p. 30.

Princess Isabel circa 1870
Joaquim Insley Pacheco
Public Domain Wikimedia Commons

The Monarchical Systems

Emancipation in Russia and Brazil took place within monarchical regimes in which monarchs not only reigned but also ruled. This had a defining influence on the process of emancipation and on its outcome. The political context differed obviously from the United States which was a republic and Britain which was a constitutional monarchy in which the monarch was a figurehead. In both Russia and Brazil, the monarch was the centre of the political system which revolved around his person. The social base of the monarchy was the master class and the basis of the alliance between the two was servile labour as we shall see. However, the closeness of interest between the two did not mean an identity of interest in all cases. That small difference created the space, potentially at least, for the two to diverge. However solicitous the emperors were to the interests of the ruling class, they were not its puppets. In both empires, the monarchs and some of its servants had a broader understanding of the interests of the state as opposed to those of the masters, who straightforwardly saw no contradiction between the two. The monarchy in Russia and Brazil possessed a degree of autonomy that allowed for independent action on the part of the monarch in certain circumstances.

The political autonomy of the monarch and a different understanding of the interests of the country proved to be the Achilles heel of the master class, opening the way for the abolition of servile labour.[52] Despite the vast differences that existed between the constitutional position of the Russian autocrat and the Brazilian emperor, the fact of a ruling monarch distinguished Russia and Brazil from other emancipations, especially in the political process. The monarchy was in some ways the *deus ex machina*, the guardian of the status quo, but also standing apart from the society over which he or she presided. It was in this space between guaranteeing the existing order and standing apart from it that opened the way to emancipation in both empires.

The Russian monarchy was an agglomeration of traditions and transformations that had created a leviathan by the end of the eighteenth century. The Muscovite or pre-Petrine monarchy was a theocratic, highly conservative institution, committed to preserving rather than transforming the society over which it presided. Peter the Great broke sharply with this tradition, secularizing the monarchy, overlaying it with a European veneer and thrusting a wholly new sense of dynamism into it. While the Russian monarchy now more closely resembled other European absolute monarchies, the limitations on absolute monarchy that existed in other European states were absent in Russia. The emperor became the 'the sole and independent source of law-making'.[53] For Peter, the monarchy was to be an agent of change, transforming the theocratic, Muscovite polity into a modern, European state.[54] The monarchy became the main agent of change, driving new innovations in technology, education, fashion and behaviour.

The power of the monarch was given definitive legal form in 1832 in the first codification of law since 1648. The Fundamental Laws of the Empire stated:

> The All-Russian Emperor is an autocratic, unlimited monarch. God himself commands obedience to his supreme autocratic power not only from fear, but also from conscience.[55]

On the issue of serfdom, theoretically at least, the maintenance of serfdom depended on the emperor's will, requiring only an assertion of will to abolish it. Catherine the Great, Alexander I and Nicholas I all considered reform or even

52 Murilo de Carvalho, *A Construção da Ordem*, p. 320.

53 Ivanova and Zheltova, *Soslovnoe Obshchestvo*, pp. 24–25.

54 Bushkovitch, *Peter the Great*, p. 12.

55 *Svod Zakonov Rossiiskoi Imperii. Tom Pervyi. Osnovnye Gosudarstvennye Zakony.* (32 vols, St. Petersburg, 1857), vol. 1, p. 1.

abolition of serfdom, yet in the end backed away for fear of the consequences. What was in question with regard to serfdom was not the power to abolish it – the Russian monarch possessed that power in abundance – but the political will. The frequent palace coups of the eighteenth and early nineteenth centuries, including the murder of Peter III in 1762 and Paul I in 1801 by disgruntled members of the nobility, were a reminder to the emperors that political realities needed to be taken into account, regardless of the theoretical extent of the monarch's powers.

In Brazil, by the time of the emancipation in 1888, the monarchy had only existed for sixty-six years. The ruling dynasty, the Braganças, was more venerable, having ruled in Portugal since 1640 when the Duke of Bragança became Dom Joao IV. The Portuguese monarchy was a scaled-down version of other absolute monarchies in Europe, concerned mainly with playing the British, French and Spanish off against each other. Nevertheless, it too had a tradition of a more activist monarchy, embodied above all by the Marquis de Pombal, the chief minister and favourite of King Dom Jose I (1756–1777). Pombal dominated the Portuguese government for the entirety of José I's reign and used his position to impose reforms on the Portuguese empire, ruthlessly crushing opposition to his plans.[56] Pombal's conception of an activist state, transforming a backward society passed, at least in part, to Brazil where the founding father of Brazilian independence Jose Andrade de Bonifacio shared Pombal's vision and wished to use a strong, activist state to abolish slavery as well effect other reforms.[57] He did not succeed, but that sense of the state as an independent actor remained, even if it was dormant for a long time.

In contrast to the Russian Empire, the Empire of Brazil was a constitutional monarchy which guaranteed basic liberal freedoms and provided a much greater public sphere. Even so, Article 101 of the Constitution of 1824 placed significant power in the hands of the emperor. He shared power with the three other pillars of the constitution: an executive, an assembly and an independent judiciary. But the Constitution also charged the emperor with overseeing the smooth operating of the system, giving him the power to intervene when necessary, the *poder moderador*. According to Articles 98-102 of the Constitution

> The *Poder Moderador* is the key to the entire political structure and is given exclusively to the Emperor as Supreme Head of the Nation and its First Representative so that he incessantly watches over the independence, equilibrium and harmony of the other Political Powers.

---

56 G. Paquett, *Imperial Portugal in the Age of Atlantic Revolutions: The Luso-Brazilian World, c. 1770–1850* (Cambridge, 2013), pp. 21–35.

57 Dolhnikov, *O Pacto Imperial*, p. 54.

Articles 101 and 102 defined the scope of the *poder moderador* which included the right to dismiss the government and dissolve the Assembly, nominate and fire ministers, appoint senators, sanction decrees and pardon criminals. The emperor was head of the armed forces, and had the right to declare war and make peace, conduct negotiations with foreign powers and make treaties.[58] However, the Constitution left the use of the *poder moderador* to the emperor's discretion, which made its use a matter of intense political controversy.[59] The Brazilian monarch did not have the blank cheque given to his Russian counterpart, but nevertheless, he had at his disposal a formidable array of powers which placed him at the centre of the political system as the Constitution stated. A great deal depended on how the emperor used those powers. Dom Pedro I's high-handed attempt to free himself from the restraints of the Constitution led to his overthrow in 1831.[60] His son Dom Pedro II was far more adept at using the powers granted to him and

Isabel and Dom Pedro II 1870
Joaquim Insley Pacheco
Public Domain Wikimedia Commons

58 http://www.planalto.gov.br/ccivil_03/constituicao/constituicao24.htm; R.J. Barman, *Brazil: The Forging of a Nation 1798–1852* (Stanford, 1988), pp. 123–26.

59 Schwarcz, *As Barbas*, p. 123; J. Needell, *The Party of Order: The Conservatives, The State and Slavery in the Brazilian Monarchy 1831–1871* (Stanford, 2006), p. 244.

60 Lustosa, *Dom Pedro* I, pp. 293–301.

dominated the political system for decades.[61] His daughter Isabel possessed the same powers when she acted as regent for him on three separate occasions.

The power of the monarch was not fully articulated by those ascribed to him under the law or constitution. Charisma in the sense that it was defined by Max Weber was an essential part of the power of the monarch and adhered to him alone. The monarch's appearance and demeanour were charged with power and meaning for both the elites and masses of the empires. In Russia, the image of the *tsar-batiuska* (little father) was one of the most powerful props of the monarchy, lasting until the Bloody Sunday massacre in St. Petersburg in 1905. The charismatic power of the Brazilian monarchy remained undiminished up to its overthrow in 1889. African traditions, such as the King of the Congo or the Day of Kings, blended with European ones to render the monarch a sacred figure.[62] Isabel's epithet, a *Redentora*, the Redeemer, which was widely used from 1887, linked her directly with Christ. This form of power was very easy to overlook, but in the words of Sean Wilentz 'nonverbal public displays and private rhetoric – political spectacle, public art, everyday gestures and remarks – can carry far more meaning and significance for contemporaries than the most eloquent, but often unread, political treatises.'[63] In both the Russian and Brazilian emancipations, these forms of power were used to overcome the intense opposition to emancipation.

Royal Women

The assumptions and values that sought to shape the lives of women in the nineteenth century placed royal women in a particularly invidious position. The eighteenth century had been rather tolerant to the exercise of power by women. The Russian Empire in the last three quarters of the century had been dominated by a series of empresses, culminating in the reign of Catherine the Great. In Portugal, Dona Maria (1777–1816), the daughter of King José I, became Queen in her own right on the death of her father in 1777. Consorts and lovers also became influential as did the aristocratic women who ran salons to which the great and the good eagerly sought invitations.

The prevailing ideas in the nineteenth century, however, were much more hostile to female rule. Twenty-five years of warfare following the French

---

61 R.J. Barman, *Citizen Emperor: Pedro II and the Making of Brazil, 1825–91* (Stanford, 1999), p. 120.

62 Schwarcz, *As Barbas*, pp. 248–48.

63 S. Wilentz, 'Introduction: Teufelsdrockh's Dilemma: On Symbolism, Politics and History' in S. Wilentz (ed), *Rites of Power: Symbolism, Ritual and Politics since the Middle Ages* (Philadelphia, 1999), p. 4.

Revolution in 1789, the masculinization of society and an increasingly sharp separation of female and male roles, enshrined in the Code Napoleon and exported all over Europe and beyond, created a much more restrictive atmosphere for the exercise of power by royal and aristocratic women. The public and private spheres were sharply separated with women excluded by law, custom and, increasingly, science from the public sphere.[64] To them was given the private world of family, the comforter of her husband and the guardians of morality. Nicholas I in Russia enthusiastically embraced these ideas. In the words of Richard Wortman, 'Nicholas played the role of knight, shielding the delicate and beautiful woman from reality. Alexandra [the empress] played the frail and exquisite damsel.'[65] In Brazil, Emperor Dom Pedro fully shared these ideals, regarding Princess Isabel and her sister Leopoldinha. Their role was that of 'radiating and emanating

Princess Isabel and her sister Leopoldina 1885
Author Unknown
Public Domain Wikimedia Commons

64 R.G. Fuchs and V.E. Thompson, *Women in Nineteenth Century Europe* (Basingstoke, 2010), p. 20.

65 R. Wortman, *Scenarios of Power: Myth and Ceremony in Russian Monarchy* (2 vols, Princeton, 1995 and 2000), vol. 1. p. 334.

maternal sweetness and gentleness', at least until the death of her last surviving brother in 1850 made Isabel the heir to the throne.[66]

For royal women, however, the bourgeois ideal of the family, predicated on a sharp separation of the public and private spheres, had little meaning in a world where everything about their lives from the cradle to the grave was public. From the great rites of passage in life to the banalities of everyday existence, they endured a life of intense and unrelenting scrutiny. Royal women were expected to embody contemporary notions of morality, but in the public gaze. They were an essential part of the power of the monarchy, a means of displaying and affirming its right to rule to itself, the elite and to the wider society. In the Russian and Brazilian empires, royal women were an indispensable part of the imagery of monarchy, just as they were in other European dynasties. In addition, they helped establish the fragile and far from universally recognized European credentials of the two empires.[67]

Both courts in the nineteenth century grew more patriarchal in tone and more hostile to female influence as the decades passed. Royal women were expected to show the same levels of obedience and deference as other women to the values of the society. Anna Tiutcheva, a lady-in-waiting at the Russian court in the 1850s, described Nicholas I's attitude to his wife, but it applied also to all the royal women: 'for him she was a charming bird whom he held in a gold and diamond studded cage.'[68] Alexander II rebuked his younger brother, Grand Duke Konstantin Nikolaevich, whose wife was thought to have too much influence on him, telling him that she should restrict herself to charitable works and warning him,'I do not permit any other kind of female interference in public affairs.'[69]

In Brazil, the attitudes of the male elite were if anything even more hostile to the exercise of female power. Most of the male elite could not come to terms with the idea of being ruled by a woman. The most hysterical denunciations of Isabel came from members of the Republican Party who regarded themselves as the bearers of modernity in Brazil. Antonio da Silva Jardim, the doyen of the Republicans, expressed most vitriolically the fears of the male elite in a series of speeches, portentously titled *A Patria em Perigo* (the Fatherland in Danger) during Isabel's Third Regency.

> She does not possess one, not one of the qualities required in order to govern. The first and original obstacle for her is her sex. Gentlemen,

---

66 Daibert , *Isabel*, pp. 34–35.

67 Wortman, *Scenarios of Power*, vol. I, p. 55; Schwarcz, *As Barbas*, pp. 109–11.

68 A. Tiutcheva, *Vospominaniia: Pri Dvore Dvukh Imperatorov* (Moscow, 2008), p. 103.

69 L. Zav'ialova and Kirill Orlov, *Velikii Kniaz' Konstantin Nikolaevich i Velikie Kniaz'ia Konstantinovichi: Istoriia Sem'i* (St. Petersburg, 2009), p. 154.

> among its wise legislation the French nation has included the Salic law which prevents a woman succeeding to the throne. It was well advised. First nature and then society through long experience which has always been justified has given to each sex its functions in the human economy: those of advice and love to the wife and of command and action to the husband. When a woman moves beyond her role – it has been said – she tarnishes her sex and is only able to become a bad man.[70]

These attitudes certainly constrained all royal women. Yet the ambiguities in the demands placed on royal women opened up spaces for them to act if they desired and possessed the intelligence and strength of character to do so. There was no shortage of role models for them to look back on. Elena had Catherine the Great as an example and the comparison was frequently made when she first arrived in Russia. One eyewitness of her first weeks in Russia enthused, 'Looking at her, I imagined that Catherine II, most likely, behaved in such a way when she was brought to the court of Elizaveta Petrovna.'[71]

Isabel came from a long line of empresses and queens. Through her grandmother, she was a direct descendent of Empress Maria-Teresa of Austria. Her great-grandmother, Dona Joaquina Carlotta was a Spanish Bourbon and a highly political, ambitious woman who openly rejected the notion that women had no place in politics. After the flight of the royal family to Brazil in 1807, there was a real possibility that Dona Carlotta would become the regent of Spanish America as the only senior member of the Spanish royal family at liberty after Napoleon had installed his brother on the throne of Spain.[72] Isabel's grandmother, Dona Leopoldinha, an Austrian Habsburg, during the War of Independence acted as regent when Dom Pedro I was away from the capital. Dona Leopoldinha fulfilled her role admirably, adroitly managing the Council of State, advising her husband and pressuring her Austrian relatives to accept Brazilian independence.[73] Her aunt, Dona Maria II (1826–1828; 1834–1853) had been Queen of Portugal in her own right during Isabel's lifetime. However, for neither woman was entry into the public sphere an easy matter. What it required was an issue

70 B. |Sobrinho (ed), *Antonio da Silva Jardim, Propaganda Republicana (1888–1889): Discursos, Opusculos, Manifestos e Artigos Coligidos* (Rio de Janeiro, 1978), pp. 58–59.

71 N.K. Shil'der, *Imperator Aleksandr Pervyi: Ero zhizn i tsarstvovanie* (4 vols, St. Petersburg, 1897), vol. 4. p. 288.

72 Pedreira and Costa, *Dom João VI* p. 235; F. Nogueira de Azevedo, *Carlota Joaquina na Corte do Brasil* (Rio de Janeiro, 2003) p. 117.

73 A. Slemian ,'O Paradigma do dever em tempos de revolução: D Leopoldina e "o sacrifício de ficar na América" ', in B. Kann, *D. Leopoldina: Cartas de Uma Imperatriz* (São Paulo, 2006), pp. 108–9.

of such fundamental importance that it overrode the normal constraints on women interfering in politics. That issue was the liberation of serfs and slaves.

Emancipation

The single most important cause of emancipation in all countries was the refusal of those in bondage to accept their condition as legitimate. No matter how long in servitude, how powerless they were before their masters, slaves and serfs always retained a vision of freedom and a more just social order.[74] Count Beckendorf, the head Nicholas I's secret police, explicitly told the emperor:

> From year to year the thought of freedom is spreading and strengthening among the peasantry. In 1834 there were many examples of disobedience of peasants to their masters, and almost all such cases, as was shown by the investigations into them, originated not in oppression nor in brutal treatment, but solely from the thought that they have a right to freedom.[75]

The master class, regardless of whatever paternal myths they created around the master/bondsman relationship, understood that the price of owning slaves was eternal vigilance and anxiety about the threat they posed. Seneca, the Roman Stoic philosopher, wrote that 'you've as many enemies as slaves'.[76] That statement was as valid in the nineteenth century as when it was written during the reign of Emperor Nero. In Russia, the Pugachev Revolt (1773–1775) remained in living memory down to the emancipation in 1861. The Haitian Revolution (1791–1804) traumatized slaveowners all over the Americas, including Brazil. In Brazil, a long indigenous tradition of resistance and revolt likewise ensured that no slave owner could ever take for granted the docility of the slaves and a major slave revolt in Salvador in 1835 disabused Brazilian slaveowners of any notion that the revolutionary threat had receded.[77] Outside of these major revolts, serfs and slaves continued to manifest their opposition to the systems of oppression, albeit in a less spectacular manner. However, the resistance of the oppressed on its own was not sufficient to win emancipation. The unquestioned legitimacy of serfdom and slavery in the wider society and the unambiguous commitment of the state, the church and the masters themselves to the serf and slave systems ensured that they endured. For emancipation to be a possibility something had to change to break this circle.

---

74 Davies, *Inhuman Bondage*, p. 35.
75 Fedorov, *Konets Krepostnichestva*, p. 61.
76 R. Campbell, *Seneca: Letters from a Stoic* (London, 2014), p. 87.
77 Reis, *Rebelião Escrava no Brasil*, pp. 68–69.

Emancipation of slaves and serfs became a live political issue in the last quarter of the eighteenth century. The transition from a passive acceptance of slavery to a fierce determination to abolish it was due above all to a transformation in moral perceptions.[78] Where slavery had previously been seen as an unfortunate but inevitable part of human existence, it was now seen as something made by humans and sustained by them through their political choices. This raised the possibility that different political choices could produce different political outcomes.[79] The delegitimization of slavery began slowly in the seventeenth century and accelerated in the eighteenth century. Enlightenment thinkers such as Kant, Voltaire, Diderot and Raynal roundly condemned serfdom and slavery. Voltaire led a famous campaign against the remnants of serfdom in France, demanding '*l'entière abolition de cette derniere trace des siècles barbarie.*'[80]

Alongside these intellectual and moral attacks on servitude, the first anti-slavery society was founded in London in 1778 by a group of Quakers. Within a generation, a tiny pressure group had transformed public opinion in Britain.[81] The mobilization of public opinion, the creation of local anti-slavery societies and the delivery of monster petitions to Parliament created a profoundly hostile climate for slavery. Previously politically inactive groups, women and the working class in England were drawn into the struggle. Women, in particular, were mobilized in their thousands by the physical and sexual abuse of female slaves by male slaveowners. For these women, moral outrage overrode the exclusion of female activity in the public sphere. Women acted not in spite of the fact that they were women, but because they were women.[82] It has been argued that the feminization of the anti-slavery struggle was a means of taking it out of politics, transferring into the realm of morality and thereby taming any potentially radical impulses.[83] However, this seems to me to be mistaken. Emancipation itself was such a radical act that no shifting of categories could tame that potential. Nor could the mobilization of women be channelled so smoothly away from any further radicalization. Mobilization on this scale and of this duration behind a single issue was unprecedented,

---

78 Davies, *Inhuman Bondage*, p. 11.

79 C.L. Brown, *Moral Capital: Foundations of British Abolitionism* (Chapel Hill, 2006), p. 153.

80 Voltaire, *Extrait d'un memoir pour l'entière abolition de la servitude em France* in *Oeuvres Complètes de Voltaire* (Paris, 1817), vol. VI, p. 204.

81 Drescher, *Emancipation*, p. 230.

82 C. Midgley, *Women against Slavery: The British Campaigns 1780–1870* (London, 1992), p. 20.

83 R.A. Kittelson, *The Practice of Politics in Postcolonial Brazil: Porto Alegre, 1845–1895* (Pittsburgh, 2006), pp. 128–34.

overcoming the seemingly impregnable defences of slavery. Under pressure from public opinion, Parliament abolished the slave trade in 1807, the first step in the abolition of slavery in the British Empire. No less important, the British state now committed itself to the interdiction of the slave trade across the globe.

Because of the ubiquity of slavery and serfdom, emancipation was an international movement from the very beginning. The American, French and Haitian Revolutions were explicitly universal in values, insisting on the equality of all human beings and in the inalienable rights that adhered to them as human beings. Such claims immediately raised the issue of serfdom and slavery, even if the authors of such claims had not always intended this.

The French Revolution deepened the attack on servile labour. On 4 August 1789, the National Assembly abolished the remnants of serfdom in France and in February 1794, under pressure from the revolutionaries in Haiti, abolished slavery in the French colonies. As the revolutionary and Napoleonic armies swept through Europe, they brought with them the same hostility to servile labour, emancipating serfs in the Rhineland states, Switzerland, the Grand Duchy of Warsaw, the Hanseatic States and Württemberg. In Prussia, the October Edict of 1807 abolishing serfdom was a direct response to the catastrophes suffered on the battlefield at Auerstead and Jena in October 1806. King Frederick William II summed up the grim mood in Prussia after the defeats: 'The abolition of serfdom has been my goal since the beginning of my reign. I desired to attain it gradually, but the disasters which have now befallen the country now justify, and indeed require, speedier action.'[84] The disintegration of Spanish authority in South and Central America and the subsequent wars of national liberation led to the abolition of slavery as all sides succumbed to the temptation to appeal to slaves to fight in return for their freedom.[85]

By the time the revolutionary era closed in 1815, serfdom and slavery had been abolished in many countries. Nevertheless, they survived in the Americas, the Caribbean and Russia. The cause of emancipation was far from won and in fact slavery in Brazil would expand rapidly as the new wonder crop of coffee generated a renewed demand for slaves first in the Paraiba Valley in Rio de Janeiro and later in São Paulo.[86] In Russia, Alexander I after some brief experiments with emancipation on the Baltic periphery decided to leave well alone and serfdom continued to flourish.

---

84 C. Clark, *The Iron Kingdom: The Rise and Downfall of Prussia 1600–1947* (London, 2006), p. 327.

85 Drescher, *Abolition*, p. 192.

86 Parron, *A Política da Excravidão*, p. 93.

Although slavery and serfdom continued to exist, and indeed thrive in some places after the Napoleonic Wars, the international context had profoundly changed. Intellectual and moral delegitimization had combined with political and military activism to bring about the end of slavery and serfdom in many parts of Europe and the Americas. No longer an inevitable part of human existence, slavery was a moral issue that greatly exercised public opinion and the policy of the most powerful state in the world, Great Britain, which committed itself to the abolition of the slave trade across the world. Brazil would experience this power directly when, under threat of bombardment of Brazilian ports by the Royal Navy, the Brazilian government finally enforced the treaties which it had signed in 1831, banning the slave trade. More subtly, the change in international opinion deeply affected the Russian and Brazilian elites. Their aspirations to be counted as part of the civilized world could not be realized as long as servile labour existed.

Conclusion

The empires of Russia and Brazil had in common European dynasties, the desire of their elites to be seen as part of what they considered to be the civilized world and, above all, their servile societies. To this in the nineteenth century was added the long struggle for emancipation. Both emancipations were part of the great wave of liberation that freed serfs and slaves everywhere and drew on the same roots of enlightenment and religious thinking. The context in which anti-slavery and anti-serfdom developed was one in which all women were excluded from the public sphere, confining them to the private sphere as guardians of morality. Slavery and emancipation, however, crossed the public/private dichotomy in a way that no other issue did. Morality mobilized women into a political struggle that lasted decades and decisively helped to end servile labour. That blurring of public and private had long been evident in the lives of royal women, whose private and family lives were played out in public as role models. Unlike in Britain or the United States, Elena and Isabel were at the heart of the power structures of their respective empires. This placed them in a unique position to act in the cause of liberation if they so wished. How they did so and with what results is the subject of the next two chapters.

Chapter 2

GRAND DUCHESS ELENA PAVLOVNA AND THE EMANCIPATION OF THE SERFS

> I said to her [Empress Maria Alexandrova] many times: we must each have our own speciality. For me now it has already been found. I have always thought about emancipation.[1]
>
> –Grand Duchess Elena Pavlona to Princess Cherkasskaia

> The Grand Duchess had the most benign influence on the course of all the important reforms which were enacted during the reign of Emperor Alexander II and especially the peasant one.... The Sovereign listened with respect to the intelligent advice and suggestions of his aunt. Using these conversations, the Grand Duchess frequently preserved the sovereign from harmful intrigues, plots and slanders.[2]
>
> –Dmitrii Miliutin (Minister of War 1861–1881)

Few could have predicted that Princess Fredericke Charlotte, the future Grand Duchess Elena Pavlovna, was destined to become one of the architects of the emancipation of serfs in the Russian Empire. Her moral framework, her intellect and her political skills made a substantial contribution not only to the ending of serfdom, but no less importantly to the conditions on which it was ended. For a woman, moreover, a foreigner, to have exercised such an influence on the most fraught and sensitive reform between the time of Peter the Great and the 1905 Revolution was a momentous achievement. Excluded by her sex from political activity, bound by the conventions of royal protocol and confronted by powerful and determined opponents,

---

1 O. Trubetskaia (ed) *Materialy dlia Biografiia kn. V.A. Cherkasskogo* (2 vols, St. Petersburg, 1901), vol. 1. p. 103.

2 D.A. Miliutin, *Vospominaniia General-Fel'dmarshala Grafa Dmitriia Alekseevicha Miliutina 1868 – nachalo 1873* (Moscow, 2006), p. 570.

Elena Pavlovna negotiated these obstacles with consummate skill to persuade the Emperor Alexander II to persevere with the emancipation and to accept one based largely on the principles favoured by her and her circle.

A combination of chance, design and circumstance placed Elena in a pivotal position in the emancipation process. A dysfunctional family, a love of learning and an unhappy marriage to a senior member of the Romanov dynasty were the chance factors that partly shaped Fredericke Charlotte's life. The circumstances that gave her that possibility were the catastrophic defeat of Russia in the Crimean War and the decision by the new Emperor Alexander II to begin the process of emancipating the serfs. The design came from Elena's momentous decision to intervene in that process, telling her friend and protege Prince Dmitrii Obolenskii 'that she had firmly resolved to try to obtain influence'.[3] These were the paths that led Elena to do what was in her power to ensure that the emancipation took place and in the form that she and her friends wanted.

Formative Influences

'I was born in Wurttemberg where my grandfather had only just become king thanks to the grace of Napoleon. I was the first child born into the now royal family'.[4] Princess Charlotte (as she was usually known) had a lonely, peripatetic childhood, deprived of any real love or affection. Her mother was an invisible presence, her largely absent father, the younger brother of the King of Wurttemberg, was boorish and had little interest in his daughter. A school friend recalled simply that 'Prince Paul, her father, was brutal'.[5] Early on, Charlotte demonstrated both a love of learning and a tenacity in achieving results that was noted by those around her.[6] Only when her father Paul decamped to Paris and packed his daughters off to boarding school did Charlotte begin to find some stability. Her early experience of school added to her misery, but through a teacher there she was introduced to the daughters of the great French scientist Georges Cuvier. Cuvier was impressed by the young Charlotte's desire for knowledge and often took

3 Obolenskii, 'Moi Vospominaniia', *Russkaia Starina*, 137 (1909), p. 524.

4 Bazhenova, 'Velikaia Kniaginia Elena Pavlovna Formirovanie Kharaktera', in Beliakov (ed), *Velikaia Kniaginia Elena Pavlovna*, p. 32.

5 K.D. Bukh, 'Velikaia Kniaginia Elena Pavlovna' *Russkaia Starina*, 57 (1888), p. 809. (Bukh's account was based on the oral testimony of a schoolfriend of Elena Pavlovna's, Madame Andre, who was educated alongside Elena in Paris.)

6 Bazhenova 'Velikaia Kniaginia Elena Pavlovna Formirovanie Kharaktera', in Beliakov (ed), *Velikaia Kniaginia Elena Pavlovna*, p. 33.

her with him on his rounds of the *Jardin des Plantes*, the botanical gardens of Paris of which he was the director.

> The extended walks through the *Jardin des Plantes*, where a wonderful collection of flora and animals was gathered, in the company of a deeply learned man such as George Cuvier, allied to the natural curiosity of the princess, contributed greatly to her maturation. He did all he could to foster her knowledge.[7]

Cuvier also presided over one of the most intellectually brilliant salons in Paris where members of the political, artistic and scientific elites gathered. Charlotte was a frequent visitor to the salon, which left a profound impression on her. Cuvier's personal approach to science and his salon embodied his belief that profundity, systematization and interconnectedness were the keys to understanding the world. Charlotte's love of knowledge was innate, but Cuvier decisively shaped her epistemological understanding which remained with her until her death. She later commented 'Here I began to love sciences and its devotees'.[8] Many decades later Prince Obolenskii, wrote 'she was always able to generalize the question and to sometimes to reach a completely unexpected conclusion, which is only characteristic of the mysterious perspicacity of the feminine mind'.[9] When Charlotte opened her own salon in St. Petersburg, Cuvier's salon was the inspiration and guiding spirit.

The Russian Court

The royal families of the numerous German states actively sought to marry into the leading dynastic families of Europe, including the Romanovs. Particularly for the smaller states, marrying a Romanov secured the family finances for at least a generation. Charlotte became part of this marriage strategy when her great aunt, the Dowager Empress Maria Fedorovna, wife of Paul I, selected Charlotte as the wife for her youngest son Mikhail Pavlovich. Princess Charlotte arrived in Russia in 1823, making favourable impressions on everybody and drawing comparisons with Catherine the Great's arrival in Russia eighty years earlier.[10] As was the custom, she converted to Orthodoxy and became Grand Duchess Elena Pavlovna.

---

7 Bukh, 'Velikaia Kniaginia Elena Pavlovna' *Russkaia Starina*, 57 (1888), p. 809.

8 Bazhenova, 'Velikaia Kniaginia Elena Pavlovna: Formirovanie Kharaktera', in Beliakov (ed), *Velikaia Kniaginia Elena Pavlovna*, p. 41.

9 Obolenskii, 'Moi Vospominaniia', *Russkaia Starina*, 137 (1909), p. 14.

10 Shil'der, *Aleksandr I*, vol. IV, pp. 287–288.

Grand Duchess Elena Pavlovna 1862
Franz Xaver Winterhalter
Public Domain Wikimedia Commons

If ever Elena had been in any doubt that for a member of the Russian royal family, the personal and political were deeply entwined, her first years in Russia would have dispelled any illusions. Even by the low standards of royal marriage, her marriage to Mikhail was a disaster. Mikhail was in love with one of his mother's ladies-in-waiting and wanted to call the wedding off.[11] Elena had little desire to marry a man who had openly declared his love for another woman, but royal marriage was an affair of state and intense pressure forced the couple to go ahead with the marriage. Mikhail's dislike for his new wife was obvious to everybody and was frequently commented upon. Empress Elizaveta Alekseevna, the wife of Alexander I, noted sadly that Elena was 'little esteemed by her spouse'.[12] The birth of Elena's first child in 1825 did nothing to improve relations, leaving Elena isolated and vulnerable. That same year to her personal trauma was added the public trauma of the Decembrist Uprising in St. Petersburg, which Elena witnessed at first-hand. For several hours,

11 Bazhenova, 'Velikaia Kniaginia Elena Pavlovna: Formirovanie Kharaktera' in Beliakov (ed), *Velikaia Kniaginia Elena Pavlovna*, p. 56.

12 D.V. Solov'ev (ed) *Elizaveta i Aleksandr: Khroniki po pis'mam Imperatritsy Elizavety Alekseevni 1792–1826* (Moscow, 2013), p. 240.

Elena and the other royal women were in fear of their lives and the lives of their children. The experience was deeply shocking for Elena, but had little impact on Mikhail's attitude to her. After the birth of her third daughter in 1828 the doctors advised her not to have any more children, ending forever the hopes of giving birth to a son and a reconciliation with Mikhail.[13] Physically and emotionally exhausted, Elena asked permission to go abroad.

Elena in Italy 1828–1829

When she left Russia for Italy in 1828, Elena was at a very low ebb. Still only twenty-two she appeared to be on the edge of a nervous breakdown. En route to Italy, she stayed with Mikhail's brother Konstantin, who was shocked by the state of the wrecked young woman.

> Her health is in a very wretched condition, but I hope that she is not altogether lost; however, it is very close to that. In her, everything has been affected, both physical and moral qualities, and the latter enormously influences the former.[...] My wife and I did our very best to bring up her morale which was at a completely low ebb.[14]

In Italy, Elena found time to take stock of her life and future. Away from the pressures of Court and a failed marriage, Elena's composure slowly returned. In a letter to Countess Nesselrode, wife of Nicholas I's foreign minister, she wrote

> I often pondered what would be our way of life after my return. In some relations we will be more free, and I would like to gather around myself a company that could give me new possibilities. I feel in this a great necessity since I'm here. I always invite a few people to dinner with whom I can exchange new ideas and who, having various jobs, offer various themes for discussion.[15]

Already in this letter, the embryo of Elena's salon can be discerned. Her broad interests, her desire to meet with people outside the normally limited court circles and her interest in new ideas were to be characteristic of her salon

---

13 Bazhenova 'Velikaia Kniaginia Elena Pavlovna: Formirovanie Kharaktera', in Beliakov (ed), *Velikaia Kniaginia Elena Pavlovna*, p. 64.

14 Jackman, 'Romanov Relations', p. 153.

15 Bazhenova, 'Velikaia Kniaginia Elena Pavlovna: Formirovanie Kharaktera', in Beliakov (ed), *Velikaia Kniaginia Elena Pavlovna*, p. 69.

in St. Petersburg. While in Italy, Elena received news of the death of the dowager Empress Maria Fedorovna, to whom she had been close. The empress in her will entrusted Elena with the management of her charitable institutions, 'knowing the kindness and firmness of her character'.[16] Elena saw in this the 'means to be useful to my country' and 'an important purpose for my life'.[17]

Elena's sojourn in Italy gave her the space to reevaluate the most important personal relationships in her life. She no longer sought to win the affection of her husband nor did she seek to win the admiration of everybody in the way

Commemorative post-card of Grand Duchess Elena Pavlovna 1912
Public Domain Wikimedia Commons
The inscription reads:
Grand Duchess Elena Pavlovna 1806–1873
Activist for the liberation of the peasanty and the founder of the clinic for the advanced training of doctors.
'She did everything that was within her power for the healing of the Russian people from the plague of legalized slavery (*rabstvo*). She firmly and emphatically supported the best Russian people of her time in their noblest strivings.'
A.F. Koni
(Note the use of the word 'slavery' by Koni, one of the greatest legal scholars and practitioners of the Imperial period.)

---

16 'Zaveshchanie Imperatritsy Marii Fedorovny' *Russkaia Starina*, 33 (1882), p. 110.

17 Bazhenova, 'Velikaia Kniaginia Elena Pavlovna: Formirovanie Kharaktera' in Beliakov (ed), *Velikaia Kniaginia Elena Pavlovna*, p. 67.

that she had done since her arrival in Russia five years earlier. She continued to fulfil her duties as a senior royal and indeed excelled at them, becoming one of the most stellar hostesses in St Petersburg. Her balls and receptions attracted universal praise. One admirer wrote that 'it would need the brush of Briulov and the pen of Pushkin to do justice to these'.[18] But Elena had also found deeper purposes for her life, desiring to be useful to her adoptive country and to return to the intellectual curiosity which she had largely abandoned since her marriage. Her engagement with any learned people passing through the court and her active pursuit of knowledge attracted both surprise and admiration in the royal family, the Emperor Nicholas remarking that 'Elena is the intellectual in our family.'[19] The management of the charitable institutions was a start, but Elena's ambitions soon went beyond this as we shall see.

Elena's World View

Elena was still only a very young woman when she returned from Italy in 1829. The journey, however, marked a watershed in the formation of her political views as much as in her personal life. In series of jottings that she wrote in Italy, she asked 'Who I am?' To which she answered 'A person free and rational, Republican by conviction, born to love my brother, And to serve my country, To live by my work and my industry, To hate slavery, And to subordinate myself to the laws'.[20] These were the principles by which she tried to live her subsequent life in Russia. Elena was both a child of the late Enlightenment, imbued with its spirit and moral purpose and a princess, acutely conscious of her position. The two elements formed the twin pillars of her political world view. In notes for her daughter, Elena wrote 'Reason is a Jacob's ladder by which we ascend from earth to Heaven and descend from Heaven to earth'.[21] For Elena, monarchy, particularly in Russia, was a progressive force. While the ideal state might be Republican, it was something for the distant future. In the here and now, the monarch, guided by reason, was the only force capable of taking the empire forward in a progressive manner. Confronted by a society marked by serfdom and a ruling class oblivious to anything but its own narrow interests, the monarchy remained the one force capable of lifting the empire out of the mire in which it was stuck. This belief in an enlightened and progressive monarchy was at the core of Elena's relationships with the most dynamic officials of her own generation and the next.

---

18 M. Korf, *Zapiski* (Moscow, 2003), p. 247.

19 Anonynmous, 'Velikaia Kniaginia Elena Pavlovna, 1806–1873', *Russkaia Starina*, 33 (1882) p. 792.

20 Reznikova, *Vel. Kn. Elena Pavlovna*, p. 46.

21 Reznikova, *Vel. Kn. Elena Pavlovna*, p. 48.

The Serf Question

Elena turned her attention to the serf question not long after her return from Italy. She shared the Enlightenment abhorrence of servile labour and soon had a chance to give practical expression of her views. Elena first became a serf mistress in 1834 when her husband presented her with an estate in Oranienbaum, one of the palace complexes not far from St. Petersburg. She became a much more substantial owner on her husband's death in 1849, inheriting his estates in Poltava in Ukraine along with 15,000 serfs.[22] Both bequests would become important testing grounds for Elena's ideas on emancipation.

The Oranienbaum estate and its contents in the words of Mikhail became 'the full and sole property of Elena'.[23] For Elena, this presented her with another opportunity to do good and to be useful. As a member of the royal family and the focus of attention, freeing the serfs was out of the question. So Elena, like many serf owners before her, sought to improve their lives in a more piecemeal fashion.

> I am completely occupied in the great matters concerning the organisation of Oranienbaum. My idea is to set up here a model farm which will in time improve the lot of the peasants. The work - which presents a lot of difficulties is at the same time interesting. I thank you for opening up for me such a wide field of useful activity.[24]

The improving serf owner was one of the stock figures of nineteenth-century Russian literature, deeply resented by the serfs who usually resisted all attempts to improve them. Elena's approach to her work drew on both the example of Cuvier and her position as a Grand Duchess. Any reform of serfdom involved intellectual, practical and ultimately political considerations, the latter particularly so because of Elena's position as a Grand Duchess. Elena began with a systematic survey of the voluminous academic and scientific literature on the problem of serfdom, much of it published in the journal of the *Free Economic Society*. Agronomic texts, statistical surveys and legal reports provided Elena with a profound understanding of the condition of the serfs. Alongside her reading Elena engaged in discussions with the leading experts on the serf question.[25]

---

22 Bakhrushin, 'Velikaia Kniaginia Elena Pavlovna', p. 139.

23 E.E. Reznikova, 'Rol' Velikoi Kniagini Eleny Pavlovny v politicheskoi zhizni Rossii' in Beliakov (ed), *Velikaia Kniaginia Elena Pavlovna*, p. 178.

24 Reznikova, 'Rol' Velikoi Kniagini Eleny Pavlovny' in Beliakov (ed), *Velikaia Kniaginia Elena Pavlovna*, p. 178).

25 Reznikova, 'Rol' Velikoi Kniagini Eleny Pavlovny' in Beliakov (ed), *Velikaia Kniaginia Elena Pavlovna*, p. 181.

Emperor Nicholas I 1850
Georg von Bothmann
Public Domain Wikimedia Commons

Most importantly, Elena became close friends with Count Kiselev, the outstanding statesman of Nicholas I's reign and the acknowledged expert on the serf question in Russia. He fully returned her admiration of him.

> This is a woman with a capacious intelligence and superior heart. One can rely absolutely on her friendship if once she confers it. Brought up under the supervision of Cuvier, a friend of her father's (Prince Paul of Wurttemberg) she remembered everything that she saw and heard in her youth.[26]

Elena focused her reform on establishing a mutually binding legal contract between the serf and the serf owner, defining the legal obligations of both. This would have ended the power of the landlord to arbitrarily increase serf obligations, significantly reducing the landlord's power. Not surprisingly,

26 Anonymous, 'Velikaia Kniaginia Elena Pavlovna *Russkaia Starina*, p. 790.

such schemes aroused intense opposition from the majority of serf owners. It bore a striking resemblance to the state-wide 'inventory' that Kiselev almost succeeded in introducing in the late 1840s. However, at the last moment, Nicholas' nerve failed him. Under the combined pressure of noble opposition and the 1848 revolutions, he abandoned the reform.

For one relatively small estate, there was no need to involve the empire's most senior official on peasant matters. Elena was only doing what many serf owners had tried to do in the past, mostly unsuccessfully. However, Elena was concerned with the broader implications of what she did. Her model farm was not just to be a model for her own serfs, but was to serve as a model for other landlords and ultimately the state itself. Cuvier's influence, as mentioned by Kiselev, and her own subsequent intellectual development always pushed her to experiment, observe, refine and then apply more broadly the results of a successful experiment. Kiselev's direct participation in the Oranienbaum experiment, ensured that the results would inform, at least partially, his own much broader plans for the reform of serfdom.[27]

Elena's attempt to improve the lives of her serfs met with mixed success. However, she drew important lessons from her own and Kiselev's experience. Firstly, the unwavering support of the sovereign was absolutely essential to any attempt to reform or abolish serfdom. Secondly, the bureaucracy and court would do everything possible to derail any reform and ruin the career of any official promoting it. Finally, the use of an outwardly private initiative to provide a model for a state-wide reform would be used again by Elena in the 1850s with her much more extensive estates in Poltava province. The drafting of the reform with the man responsible for peasant affairs in the Empire would be repeated by Elena twenty years later when her friend and protege Nikolai Miliutin drafted an emancipation project for her extensive estates in Poltava province. Elena had also accumulated a vast amount of legal, technical and practical expertise regarding serfdom and its reform which few other people possessed. The failure of Kiselev's reform gave Elena a sharp lesson in the dark arts employed by the opponents of emancipation. She understood that there was an intense political battle to be waged which had to be won or any attempt to reform, let alone abolish, serfdom was doomed. Under the more propitious conditions of Alexander II, this was to prove critical in allowing Elena to help shape the emancipation.

---

27 Reznikova, *Vel. Kn. Elena Pavlovna*, pp. 60–61.

Alexander II 1873
Nikolai Lavrov
Public Domain Wikimedia Commons

Elena and Young Officials

Royal women in both Muscovy and Imperial Russia had long been accustomed to seeking favours for family members, friends and those they felt had been wronged.[28] All royal women in the nineteenth century could act in this way without arousing hostility or anger at interfering in something that was normally in the sphere of men. Royal women's intervention, subverting the usual bureaucratic lines of command, was a small but significant assertion of autocratic power over the routines of the bureaucracy. Rather than threatening the male preserve of public power, it confirmed long-established gender roles.

However, in the 1840s Elena began to use this traditional power in an unusual way. Instead of obtaining favours for disparate individuals, Elena began to sponsor a group of young officials working in the various ministries. What these officials had in common was intelligence, drive and a commitment to reform. Through her various contacts with senior officials, Elena began to invite these young men to her palace and later to her salon. Prince Obolenskii, a bright young official in the Ministry of Justice, was among

28 I. Thyrêt, *Between God and the Tsar: Religious Symbolism and the Royal Women of Muscovite Russia* (Dekalb, Illinois, 2001), p. 79.

the very first who came to her attention and it was on his second meeting with Elena that he began to understand why he had been summoned.

> Speaking about the younger generation, she expressed to me all her sympathy for its noble impulses and strivings. She spoke with indignation of the emptiness and pettiness of court life, of the absence of thought, of any desire to find out and understand the needs of the country, about the general indifference, the empty lifeless formalism ruining everything. She emphasized the sincerity of her words by animated gestures and with the unfeigned expression of her shining flashing eyes.[29]

Many other young officials received invitations to visit Elena, including the Miliutin brothers, Nikolai and Dmitrii; the former would eventually draft the emancipation legislation. Elena's use of her station to sponsor and protect the careers of a particular group of young officials considerably stretched the traditional royal prerogative of doing individual favours based largely on whim. She was pushing the limits of what was permissible for female members of the royal family to do, extending her patronage to promote a faction based on their reformist orientation. Her sponsorship of these young men was to prepare them for the moment when reform was possible, as Elena was evidently convinced would happen. Despite her close friendship with the emperor Nicholas, Elena was not blind to the problems facing the empire and the failure of the existing regime to deal with them. She looked to these young men to be in place when that moment came.

The Salon of Elena Pavlovna

By the mid-1840s, Elena was a very different person from the young girl who had arrived in Russia in 1823 and the deeply unhappy woman who had left Russia to travel to Italy in 1828. Elena herself had changed, becoming self-confident, authoritative and assertive. She was a part of Nicholas' inner circle and their mutual friendship, not without its ups and downs, deepened with time. She was one of the few women that he respected intellectually.[30] On a personal level, Elena's relationship with her husband had become one of mutual respect if not close. Tragedy struck Elena in the mid-1840s when her two eldest daughters both died in childbirth within a year of each other. Shortly after the death of her second daughter in 1846, Elena decided to

---

29 Obolenskii, 'Moi Vospominaniia', *Russkaia Starina* 137 (1909), p. 510.

30 Reznikova, 'Rol' Velikoi Kniagini Eleny Pavlovny' in Beliakov (ed), *Velikaia Kniaginia Elena Pavlovna*, p. 177.

open her own salon in St. Petersburg. Presenting the salon as a low key affair designed to allow her last surviving daughter to meet with suitable people, the Thursday night salon in the Mikhailovskii Palace soon became one of the highlights of the social calendar.

There was nothing particularly unusually about an aristocratic salon, even one run by women of the royal family. The Empresses Maria Fedorovna and Alexandra Fedorovna both had salons that were part of the social life of the Court. However, Elena did not want to create yet another space for courtiers to meet to exchange gossip. Instead, she looked to the salons of the Bourbon restoration in Paris and particularly those of her great mentor Georges Cuvier. To her salon would be invited those who were distinguished by achievement rather than birth. The guests - artists, writers, musicians statesmen, diplomats-reflected closely the salons of her time in Paris. Contemporary issues, international relations, literature were all discussed at the salon. There were even readings from Alexander Herzen's newspaper *Kolokol*, published in London and forbidden in Russia.[31] The Emperor Nicholas himself often attended (presumably not when *Kolokol* was being read.) Merely by placing the emperor and other members of the imperial family with people from outside the usual court circles in the same space, Elena was expanding the parameters of what was considered acceptable for a female member of the royal family to do. Her friend Count Kiselev remarked that the breach of protocol did not go unnoticed.

> The guests did not always belong to the highest circles of society. It was personal achievement that was taken into account with these guests. This offended those who put rank above all else and who were scandalized by any liberal act, however distinguished or splendid the guest might be.[32]

Elena had no overtly specific political purpose to the salon, but, inevitably, the regular gathering of so many influential people from the political, cultural, intellectual and diplomatic elites made it a numinous place. As a Grand Duchess and intimate of the emperor, her invitations had great power. The magnificent setting of the Mikhailovskii Palace, in the very centre of St Petersburgh, enhanced the aura of power around the salon. In themselves, the hostess, the guests and the setting created a space that had political potential. The frequent presence of the emperor, moreover, infused the salon with political energy and consequence. It was in a conversation with the British ambassador at one of Elena's soirees that Nicholas called the Ottoman Empire 'the sick man

31 Bakhrushin, 'Velikaia Kniaginia Elena Pavlovna', p. 159.
32 Anonymous, 'Velikaia Kniaginia Elena Pavlovna', p. 792.

of Europe', words that caused such alarm in London.[33] Nicholas' attendance was in some ways surprising, given that its existence could be taken as a veiled criticism of his regime and policies. His close friendship with Elena was one explanation for his participation; another was that Nicholas was a great lover of music and a talented musician and immensely enjoyed Elena's musical evenings. Anton Rubenstein, one of the giants of Russian classical music in the nineteenth century, was a regular at the salon:

> The musical-artistic evenings at the Grand Duchess Elena Pavlovna's were extraordinarily interesting. Here were gathered positively the very best artists who were in St. Petersburg. The majestic figure of the Emperor Nikolai Pavlovich was often among the guests. The sovereign was always well disposed to me. This kindness was expressed by his attention, with a few kind words. But on one occasion at the Grand Duchess's the Sovereign Nikolai Pavlovich sat alongside me for an very long time at the piano and with wonderful skill whistled an entire opera.[34]

Grand Duchess Elena Pavlovna 1822
Felice Schiavoni
Public Domain Wikimedia Commons

33 Obolenskii, 'Moi Vospominaniia', *Russkaia Starina*, 137 (1909) p. 516.
34 A. Rubenstein, 'Vospominaniia Antona Grigorovicha Rubensteina', *Russkaia Starina*, 64 (1889), p. 543.

The thirty years separating Elena's arrival in Russia from the outbreak of the Crimean War in 1853 provided a long, and at times bitter, apprenticeship in the ways of the Russian royal family and Court. Elena had experienced an unhappy marriage, the terrible loss of two of her three adult children and a court role that was vacuous and devoid of meaning. Nevertheless, she had succeeded in building a life for herself that more closely reflected her own interests and desires. Her charitable works, her cultivation of intellectual contacts and her experimentation with peasant reforms in Oranienbaum had given meaning to her life. Those different threads of her life came together in her salon in the late 1840s. The bruising personal experiences of her life in Court, particularly her first ten years, had hardened Elena and given steel to her character. These personal experiences of Elena were also public ones. The Court was apex of the political system, the emperor the point at which all forces converged. Despite her dislike of the Court, Elena fully understood its power and the ways in which that power was exercised by the emperor and by those who sought to influence him. It operated under rules that were hidden from outsiders and strewn with pitfalls even for knowledgeable insiders. Elena's thirty years of experience in the court and her shrewd political brain gave her an unrivalled mastery of the Court and its ways. That would be tested like never before in the great crisis that began in 1853 and continued until 1861.

The Crimean War 1853–1856

The Crimean War was one of the great watersheds of Russian history. It destroyed the Russian Empire's reputation as the world's leading military power, it traumatized the Russian elite and it opened the way for the most radical transformation of Russian society before the 1917 revolutions. The centrepiece of that transformation was the emancipation of the serfs, occurring five years after the end of the disastrous war. Nicholas I died in 1855 in the midst of the war and was succeeded by his son Alexander. Widely regarded as weak and lacking backbone, it would be Alexander II who would succeed in liberating the serfs where Catherine the Great, Alexander I and Nicholas I failed.[35] Yet the path from defeat to emancipation was neither direct nor clear. Alexander himself had no plan or idea of how to bring it about. Nor was there any comparable example to draw on.

35 S.S. Tatishchev, *Imperator Aleksandr II : Ego Zhizn' i Tsarstvovanie* (2 vols, St. Petersburg, 1903), vol. 1, p. 34.

The emancipations brought by the revolutionary wars were clearly not acceptable. The only remotely relevant example was the Prussian emancipation of 1807, also inspired by catastrophic military failure. But it was indeed remote. Serfdom was not central to Prussia in the way it was to Russia; Prussian society was more diverse, the economy more complex and the political system more open.

Elena and the Crimean War

The Crimean War opened the possibility for Elena to broaden her field of activity in a way impossible to imagine before the war. News of the scandalous state of Russian military hospitals had shocked Russian society. In response, Elena, working closely with one of Russia's outstanding surgeons Dr Pirogov, set up the Russian Sisters of Mercy, a nursing unit to take care of the wounded soldiers.[36] It was a bold act for a female member of the royal family to take, interfering directly in the army, the institution that was the essence of the masculine sphere and a personal fetish of every male Romanov. It was no easy matter for Elena to persuade Nicholas and the senior military to accept her proposals. But given the manifest failures of the existing system and Elena's determination the emperor acquiesced.[37]

These changes reflected a deeper change taking place within the political system. The Emperor Nicholas' confidence was shattered by the unfolding catastrophe in the Crimea. Although he kept up the facade of the all-powerful, all-confident autocrat, he was beginning to break under the strain. His iron grip on his family and the empire itself was loosening. The person he turned to for emotional support was Elena and in the last two years of his life, he was a frequent visitor to the Mikhailovskii Palace.[38] It was during one of these visits that he confided to Elena that 'perhaps his son would succeed in carrying out his desire to free the peasantry from serfdom, which he himself had failed to do'.[39] Nicholas' confession was the spur that Elena needed to move from the realm of private activity of a benign serf owner to the public sphere of actively seeking a general emancipation. On the day after Nicholas' death, Elena told Prince Obolenskii that she had firmly decided 'to try

---

36 N.A. Beliakov and V.A. Mikhailovich, 'Krestovozdvizhenskaia Obshchina' in Beliakov (ed), *Velikaia Kniaginia Elena Pavlovna*, p. 124.

37 Obolenskii, 'Moi Vospominaniia', *Russkaia Starina*, 137 (1909), p. 518.

38 Semenov Tian-Shanskii, *Memuary* vol. III, p. 95.

39 Semenov Tian-Shanskii, *Memuary* vol. III p. 95.

to obtain influence'.[40] Petr Semenov Tian-Shanskii, her friend and one of the architects of the emancipation, wrote

> From this time the grand duchess regarded herself as the most faithful defender of the great idea of the liberation of the peasantry and strengthened her intention to move, in favourable circumstances, to a more active role in the unavoidable renewal of Russia through a whole series of reforms.[41]

The Opening of Politics

Elena did not have long to wait for favourable circumstances. From the beginning of the reign rumours began to circulate about the new emperor's intention to emancipate the serfs.[42] Alexander addressed these rumours directly in a speech to representatives of the Moscow nobility in March 1856.

> I know, gentleman, that amongst you rumours are spreading about my intention to abolish serfdom. In rejecting various unfounded rumours on such an important subject, I regard it as necessary to say to you all that I have no intention to do this now. But, of course, you yourselves understand that the existing order of the ownership of souls cannot remain unchanged. Better to begin abolition of serfdom from above than to wait for the time it will begin to abolish itself from below. I ask you gentleman to consider how to put this into practice. Pass on my words to the nobles for consideration.[43]

Alexander's call to the nobility to consider this problem marked a radical departure from all previous practice regarding emancipation in which any consideration was shrouded in the deepest secrecy. Along with the call, the absence of any concrete proposals was a telling indication that Alexander had no idea how to proceed. So, just like his father, he set up another secret committee to examine the issue of emancipation. For Elena, though, Alexander's call to the nobility to think about ways in which

40 Obolenskii, 'Moi Vospominaniia', *Russkaia starina* 137 (1909), p. 524
41 Semenov Tian-Shanskii *Memuary*, vol. III, p. 96
42 Tatishchev, *Imperator Aleksandr II*, p. 302
43 Tatishchev *Imperator Aleksandr II*, p. 302

emancipation might be brought about was the chance she had been waiting for. As a substantial serf owner, she could now legitimately consider ways to abolish serfdom.

There were many schemes for emancipation. The majority of nobles were against any emancipation in general, but if forced to accept one, they wanted an emancipation in which the peasantry became landless labourers and utterly dependent on their former masters.[44] This was essentially the emancipation that had taken place in the Baltic provinces in 1819. For the government this was unacceptable, posing a real threat to stability of the empire. There were also many proposals that were more favourable to the peasantry, involving ending the judicial power of the landlord over the serf, emancipating peasants with land and paying compensation to the former masters. It was this more generous or liberal emancipation that Elena and her circle favoured.

Unlike many of those who now produced schemes for abolition, Elena had two decades of dense experience to draw on. With her close friend, Nikolai Miliutin, she began to draw up a detailed plan for transforming Alexander's appeal into specific proposals. Elena's plan was focused this time on her 15,000 serfs on the Karlovka estates and was based on three broad principles. The judicial power of the landlord over the peasants was to be ended, the peasants were to be freed with land and the nobles were to receive financial compensation for their land from the peasants.[45] The broad principles of Elena's plan were not new; an emancipation on these lines had long been discussed. What was new was that Elena's plans were laid out in precise detail and in the formal language of the state bureaucracy, which put them far in advance of any other proposals. [46]Although Elena presented her reform as that of a private citizen, her ambition extended beyond her the serfs on her own estate. Her attempts at reform twenty years earlier with Kiselev had also been drawn up with a much wider application in mind. Now in the radically changed conditions of the new reign, she wanted to provide a blueprint for the entire emancipation, bypassing the bureaucracy completely.[47] The final terms of the emancipation closely resembled those put forward by Elena in her Karlovka project, hardly surprising considering that Nikolai Miliutin was the main draftsman of the Karlovka scheme and of the final Emancipation Act in 1861. However, when she presented her proposals to Alexander in late 1856, he was taken aback by how radical they were and rejected them, preferring to wait for the bureaucracy to come

44 Blum, *Lord and Peasant in Russia*, p. 581.

45 Bakhrushin, 'Velikaia Kniaginia Elena Pavlovna', pp. 140–142.

46 Lincoln, 'The Karlovka Reform', pp. 463–471.

47 Bakhrushin, 'Velikaia Kniaginia Elena Pavlovna', p. 141.

up with proposals for the emancipation.[48] The next five years were devoted not so much to changing the plan, but to changing Alexander's attitude to the one presented by Elena. It was here that Elena's knowledge of Alexander, court politics and the methods of her political enemies provided the reformers with the critical advantage over their opponents.

Elena and the committed group of young bureaucrats around her had little faith that the bureaucracy would come up with any workable proposals. True to form, the secret committee set up to examine the issue of emancipation reported nine months later that, although reform was desirable, nothing could be done for the present.[49] It was precisely at this point that all previous attempts to reform serfdom under Nicholas I had ran aground. His father had never got beyond this stage and few expected Alexander to have the strength of character to override the bureaucracy. Yet here contingency turned events in a different direction. Alexander refused to accept that nothing could be done and sought a way out of the deadlock. It was provided by V.A. Nazimov, the governor of the provinces of Vilna, Grodno and Kovno, who in 1857 petitioned Alexander for permission to set up committees of nobles of his provinces to present proposals for emancipation. Alexander granted permission in what became known as the Nazimov Rescript. Soon after similar rescripts were published for other provinces. The rescripts publicly committed the government to emancipation for the first time, from which there could be no turning back.[50] No, less importantly, Alexander had taken the responsibility for reform out of the dead hands of the bureaucracy. Elena and her circle saw this unexpected development as the chance they had been waiting for.[51] The first and most significant battle had been won. What was at stake now was the type of emancipation that would be produced.

The Editing Commission 1859–1860

From 1857 proposals from various noble committees flooded into the government. To process these and formulate legislation based on them, Alexander set up an ad hoc commission composed of bureaucrats and experts in the field. He did this following the advice of General Iakov Rostovtsev, his most trusted advisor and a recent convert to emancipation.[52] Alexander appointed Rostovtsev head of the Commission and gave him a free hand in appointing its members.

48 Obolenskii, 'Moi Vospominaniia', *Russkaia Starina*, 138 (1909), pp. 38–39.
49 Tatishchev, *Imperator Aleksandr II*, vol. I, p. 284–286.
50 Field, *End of Serfdom*, pp. 89–94.
51 Obolenskii, 'Moi Vospominaniia', *Russkaia Starina*, 143 (1909) p. 42.
52 Tatishchev, *Imperator Aleksandr II*, vol. I, pp. 319–320.

The Editing Commission, as it was called, was far more than its rather bland name implied. It was to consist of representatives of the ministries and outside experts. The Commission had no legal or institutional basis, but had been ordered into existence by the emperor and was directly subordinated to him.[53] This was simultaneously its great strength and weakness. As long as the emperor supported the Commission, it would be impervious to attacks from the bureaucracy and the Court, but if that support was undermined, the Commission would collapse immediately. The members of the thirty-seven man commission were chosen by Rostovtsev, guided by Nikolai Miliutin and the reformist brother of the emperor, Grand Duke Konstantin Nikolaevich. As far as possible they chose men who were committed to emancipation, although they had to include several known opponents of it. The Committee, however, was dominated by those who were advocates of emancipation. All of these were, or soon became, close friends of Elena.[54] They shared her vision of a radical emancipation and did all they could to ensure that it was this version that would triumph. The Commission, however, had many enemies in the bureaucracy and the Court. It was the latter that were to be particularly feared since the vast majority opposed any type of emancipation and were determined to block it. As members of his Court, his personal suite and hunting cronies they had direct and constant access to the Alexander. They were past masters in the game of court politics and knew exactly how to play on Alexander's fears and neurosis and undermine his faith in the Commission. He himself confessed his feeling of isolation in regard to emancipation.[55] One of Elena's closest friends, Prince Dmitrii Obolenskii wrote of the acute danger that the Commission faced from its Court opponents and its vulnerability to the mood of emperor, 'the guiding will'.

> The opposition was not open nor did it have any obvious center. Nevertheless, it was dangerous owing to the absence of confidence in the firmness of the guiding will. We were constantly afraid of the direction that the final outcome of the reform would be given by the main members of the Editing Commission. Everything that hatred, malice, and slander could devise for the defamation of these members and to impute to them the charge of political unreliability was done.[56]

53 L.G. Zakharova, *Aleksandr II i Otmena Krepostnogo Prava v Rossii* (Moscow, 2011) p. 213.

54 Reznikova, 'Rol' Velikoi Kniagini Eleny Pavlovny' in Beliakov (ed), *Velikaia Kniaginia Elena Pavlovna*, p. 229.

55 Tatishchev, *Imperator Aleksandr II*, vol. 1, p. 282.

56 Obolenskii, 'Moi Vospominaniia', *Russkaia Starina* 143 (1909), p. 60.

Elena's Strategy

Elena and her circle were acutely aware of the danger to the Commission from this quarter. Elena took upon herself the task of ensuring the safety of the Commission and the nullifying of attempts by its enemies to undermine it. She provided advice, emotional support and placed one of her palaces on Elaginskii Island at the disposal of the Editing Commission, which became its unofficial headquarters. She took on herself the unglamorous, but essential task of ensuring that the core members of the Commission did not fall out, but remained united and focused on their goal of a radical emancipation.

> She understood that bringing people together who were estranged for various reasons required an intermediary. Nobody could fulfil the role of intermediary better than her. She took this on herself and put the whole force of her charming intelligence to this end.[57]

Elena also understood the fragile male egos she was dealing with in the Editing Commission. Even though they all shared a broadly similar view of the emancipation, there was no guarantee that disagreement on points of detail would not wreck the work of the Commission. In a long conversation with Prince Cherkasskii, a leading member of the Commission, and his wife Princess Cherkasskaia, Elena emphasised 'the main thing is to be unified in all matters and in everything that is to reach the sovereign. If you do not preserve your unity, they will shoot you down from all sides like wild beasts and you will achieve nothing'.[58] Around Elena were gathered a small group of women who formed part of Elena's core strategy. Elena recognized that there were occasions when 'a woman could perhaps do more than a man'.[59] These women included her daughter Ekaterina Mikhailovna, her lady-in-waiting Baroness Raden, Princess Cherkasskaia and Maria Miliutina wife of Nikolai Miliutin. Baroness Raden explained to Princess Cherkasskaia 'that it is necessary that your sacred battalion does not disintegrate even from the point of view of where you live, and the island must remain its headquarters'.[60] These women acted tirelessly as go-betweens, fixers and troubleshooters. This unseen, patient and determined work was deeply political. It took traditional female attributes of the comforter, supporter and provider of solace, repurposing them to serve political ends. At all times, focus on the goal remained paramount. It gave a sense of unity and purpose to the members of the Editing Commission that their opponents lacked.

---

57 Obolenskii, 'Moi Vospominaniia', *Russkaia Starina* 143 (1909), p. 58.

58 Trubetskaia, *Materialy*, p. 26.

59 Trubetskaia, *Materialy*, pp. 26–27.

60 Trubetskaia, *Materialy*, p. 58.

In Imperial Russia ministers were nominally powerful, controlling the bureaucracies that ran the empire. However, a parallel power structure existed around the person of the emperor that could render formal titles meaningless. In this sphere, the voice, gestures, demeanour of the emperor towards individuals or groups were the currency of power, determining who needed to be taken seriously and who could be ignored. When Nikolai Miliutin was first introduced to Alexander, the emperor spoke politely to him, but his dislike for Miliutin was evident in the tone of his voice. Miliutin's wife Maria recalled that 'the tone clearly stunned my husband' and he seriously considered resigning.[61] Even if in the nineteenth century there were no favourites comparable to Prince Menshikov under the Peter the Great or to Grigori Rasputin under Nicholas II (1895–1917), those close to the emperor physically were in a unique position to influence policy.

Elena understood that the Editing Commission's success or failure depended entirely on Alexander's attitude to it. Although he had set up the Commission, Alexander kept his distance from it. The Editing Commission, apart from General Rostovtsev, was made up of men who no access to the emperor. Elena wanted Alexander to engage directly with members of the Commission so that he could judge them for himself rather than through the filter of those who sought to destroy it. Yet access to the emperor was no easy matter. Thickets of protocol surrounded access to the person of the emperor, which even a member of the royal family could not easily ignore. A brusque introduction to Alexander would likely offend him, particularly if he felt that it was part of an attempt to influence him. The Grand Duchess coached her friends in the esoteric ways of the Court, helping them to avoid obvious errors. Elena understood her nephew's insecurities very well, warning Prince Cherkasskii that 'the Sovereign fears any direct interference – he is jealous of his power'.[62] Bringing the members of the Commission into the presence of the emperor in a way that did not offend him would constitute a major, if incomplete, victory for Elena and the Commission.

Elena's Salon

The means by which Elena would provide access to the emperor was her salon. This was the only space in which she could bring the emperor and the members of the commission together as her guests. Her Thursday

---

61 M. A. Miliutina, 'Iz zapisok Marii Ageevny Miliutinoi', *Russkaia Starina*, 97 (1899), p. 51.
62 Trubetskaia, *Materialy*, p. 26

evenings had long been a highlight of the social calendar in St. Petersburg. Elena subtly expanded the attractions of the evenings to include less cerebral activities such as card playing, charades and dancing, which were more to Alexander's taste than weighty intellectual discussions. Alexander began to attend the salon from 1855 onwards and became a regular attendee. His mood was invariably good when he was there. Princess Cherkasskaia wrote in her diary on 3 March 1860. 'There were games of catch. The Sovereign was very jolly watching the games and was laughing with all his heart'.[63] His presence in the salon now made it a locus of power where political where political agendas could be contested, which was Elena's intention. Prince Obolenksii disclosed the overtly political nature of Elena's salon between 1858 and 1861, the period between the formation of the Editing Commission and the Emancipation Proclamation.

> The most important members of the Editing Commission were always among the guests. With astonishing skill the hostess was able to group her guests in such a way to attract the attention of the emperor and empress and to engage them in conversation with people who were frequently not to their taste and against whom they might have been warned. Moreover, this was all done in such a way that it was unnoticeable to those eyes that were not party to the secret and without exhausting the sovereign, who found great pleasure in the diversity of these evenings.[64]

Even though the emperor and the members of the Commission were in the same space, they could not simply walk up to the emperor and begin a conversation. Elena carefully choreographed the evenings to ensure the members of the commission attracted the attention of the emperor as Obolenskii stated. She was aided in this by her female friends who moved through the salon, acting as her eyes and ears. The women passed easily between the different circles and spaces of the salon, seeking always to bring together the emperor and Elena's friends on the Commission. When it happened, they lost no time in informing Elena: 'In such cases (which were repeated later) m-lle Eiler and Edith as well flew to the grand duchess and said quietly, "H. M. is speaking to the prince or is looking for Mr. Milutine," and our benevolent hostess rejoiced and tried to arrange things so that nobody interfered in the conversation.'[65]

---

63 Trubetskaia, *Materialy*, p. 154.

64 Obolenskii, 'Moi Vospominaniia', *Russkaia Starina*, 143 (1909), pp. 59–60.

65 Trubetskaia, *Materialy*, p. 127.

In this supposedly neutral space, Elena could arrange, as if by chance, for the emperor to meet with her friends on the Commission, talk with them and get to know them first-hand rather than through the filter of those who hated them. Such introductions and conversations were important in themselves, but they were public displays of the emperor's attention and goodwill which was not lost on the onlookers. Princess Cherkasskaia recalled one such conversation between her husband and the emperor, illustrating perfectly the dual functions of any conversation with the emperor.

> At first the sovereign spoke a few words with me, but then for much longer with the prince about the commission. He sat down beside him in order to speak with him and this produced a singular impression on the public and some impression on us as well.[66]

Elena's salon was the only place members of the Commission could receive the emperor's affirmation, not so much by what he said, but through being seen talking to them. Elena's use of her salon for this purpose nullified the advantage of exclusive access to the emperor that opponents of the emancipation had previously enjoyed. The success of Elena's tactic was acknowledged by her enemies at court. A frustrated Prince A.F. Orlov blurted out to the emperor 'I can't bear what happens in that house'.[67] More measured but no less bitter testament came from another enemy of emancipation N.A. Mukhanov

> Several of them (supporters of the emancipation) had gained access to the imperial family at her salon and they had easy access to it and spoke freely about this present matter. Not only did they enjoy the advantage over those who did not share their opinion, but they constantly avoided conversations with them.[68]

What remained, however, was still to get the emperor to embrace the emancipation proposed by Elena and her friends on the Commission. As aunt of the emperor and with an unrivalled knowledge of Alexander accumulated over decades, Elena was better placed than anybody else to accomplish this delicate mission.

---

66 Trubetskaia, *Materialy*, p. 127.
67 Bakhrushin, 'Velikaia Kniaginia Elena Pavlovna', p. 163.
68 Bakhrushin, 'Velikaia Kniaginia Elena Pavlovna', p. 163.

Elena and Alexander

Alexander II was at all times the key figure in the emancipation. From beginning to end it was his desire for emancipation that made it possible. However, Alexander did not know what emancipation he wanted nor how he could achieve it. Elena knew precisely what type of emancipation she wanted and how to achieve it. Her task was to persuade Alexander to accept the version of emancipation favoured by her circle and, once persuaded, make sure that he stuck to it. That was no easy matter. Alexander had been close to Elena when he had been a little boy, but as an adult she did not have a particularly close relationship with him and he, like most of the family, regarded his intellectual aunt as something of an oddity.[69] Alexander was also extremely sensitive to his prerogatives as emperor, well aware that he did not command the same authority as his father. Elena's remark that 'he [Alexander]is jealous of his power' applied particularly to women.[70] Elena had to be extremely careful in how she engaged with Alexander and his brittle male ego.

Her personal relationship with Alexander developed too. Little by little Alexander began to listen to his aunt on the subject of emancipation, discussing the details of the process with her and increasingly the politics. In 1857 he met with Elena and the renowned German specialist Baron Von Haxhausen to discuss various emancipation proposals. When the head of the Commission, Count Rostovtsev died of cancer midway through its work, Alexander appointed Count Panin, a known reactionary as its new head. Elena was distraught by this appointment and protested to Alexander. The emperor reassured her that 'Panin in general has no convictions and his only concern will be to please me'.[71] What was surprising was that Alexander felt the need to explain to his aunt a political decision and was a mark of how the relationship between the two had developed. The Editing Commission finished its work in 1860 and handed over its detailed recommendations to the bureaucracy for its final passage into law. The main proposals of the Editing Commission as broadly formulated in Elena's Karlovka project made it through the final stages of the legal process substantially intact. If the main credit for the emancipation belongs to Alexander himself, Elena and her friends determined the shape of that emancipation in no small measure.

The Emancipation Act of 1861 was a remarkable achievement, bringing to an end serfdom in Russia and providing the basis for the radical transformation

---

69 Obolenskii, 'Moi Vospominaniia', *Russkaia Starina*, 137 (1909), p. 524.

70 Trubetskaia, *Materialy*, pp. 26–27.

71 Miliutina, 'Iz zapisok', *Russkaia Starina*, 98 (1899), p. 125.

of Russian society. Peasants were freed from the judicial power of their lords permanently and they received land from their masters, although as community rather than as individuals. Emancipation with land sharply distinguished emancipation in the Russian Empire from that in Britain, the United States and Brazil where the former slaves received nothing. However, peasant freedom was conditional and the peasants were now subject to their own communal institutions rather than the whim of their old masters. Even if this was less arbitrary and more tolerable than the judicial power of the noble, it still rankled. Most resented of all, however, was the indemnity the peasantry had to pay for the land they received, a process spread over the next forty-nine years. This offended the deepest peasant belief that the land belonged to them. The loss of access to meadows, pastures, woods and waterways only added to the sense of grievance, which was passed down the generations, bearing bitter fruit in 1905 and 1917. Peasants belonging to the state had to wait until 1866 for their freedom, when they were freed under similar conditions, but with more land. The vast majority of nobles deeply resented the terms of emancipation and felt betrayed by the emperor and the state. Not surprisingly, given their irreconcilable visions of emancipation, no settlement could have satisfied both peasant and noble. The compromise pleased no one and stored up problems for future. However, the emancipation did provide the basis for a radical transformation of the empire, which was partially achieved in the coming decades. The problems created by the emancipation were not insoluble and could have been resolved with political will and flexibility. The failure to do so was not the fault of the original emancipators, but that is another story.

Elena and the Great Cause

Elena and the men and women who made up her circle were not naïve idealists who supported emancipation solely for moral reasons. The men in it had either made brilliant careers in state service such as Count Kiselev or Baron Korf or would go on to make them such as the Miliutin brothers and Prince Obolenskii. The women, such as Baroness Raden or Maria Miliutina, were all highly educated, cultured and deeply interested in the development and the future of the empire. They understood perfectly well the pragmatic reasons for emancipation such as the long-term security of the state, the modernization of the army and the need for a root-and-branch reform of the empire and its institutions in general. Emancipation was the essential first step towards these larger goals. However, it was not pragmatism that was at the root of what they did during the years 1856–1861.

Elena and her circle saw themselves engaged in an epic moral drama similar to those who fought for emancipation in Britain and the Americas.

The language they routinely used between themselves reverberated with this understanding of what they were doing. Emancipation was referred to as the 'Great Idea' (*Velikaia Ideia*),[72] the core of the Editing Commission was the 'Sacred Battalion', as we have seen, and Elena herself became the 'Mother-Benefactress'.[73] At Christmas 1859, a particularly difficult time for the Commission, Elena sent Miliutin a photo album inscribed with a verse from Psalm 126: *They that sow in tears, shall reap in joy.*[74] The psalm had been written to celebrate the deliverance of the Jews from Babylonian captivity, a telling allegory for the work of the Commission. A still more revelatory sense of how Elena and her friends conceptualized themselves and their work came when the chairman of the Editing Commission, Rostovtsev, was dying. Elena and Princess Cherkasskaia spoke about him, drawing on the story that had sustained generations of the oppressed in resistance to servility. On the eve of Rostovtsev's death in January 1860, Princess Cherkasskaia wrote:

> Yesterday I dined at the Grand Duchess' alone. She was very anxious. 'I have always thought that Rostovtsev will be like Moses. He will not see the promised land and in this way will expiate the sins of his youth'.
> 'Will we see it madame?'
> 'Why not?' she replied with passion.[75]

Positioning herself and her circle within the Exodus narrative was not hyperbole or vanity, but reflected the sense of mission that was driving them and was at the root of what they did. In choosing Exodus, Elena was identifying her group with the oldest and most potent liberation story of all, just as the countless multitude of others who fought for emancipation in Europe and the Americas had done and would continue to do. The exalted language and metaphor reflected the uniqueness of emancipation as a moral struggle, elevating it beyond any other issue. After the Emancipation, a whole series of momentous reforms followed, known collectively as the Great Reforms, which set the empire on a radically new trajectory. Elena followed them closely and with intense interest, but she made no attempt to influence them.[76] It was the uniqueness of emancipation that pushed Elena openly to cross the line separating women from politics. In doing so, she profoundly influenced the emancipation of the serfs in Russia.

---

72 Tian-Shanskii, *Memuary*, p. 96.
73 Trubetskaia, *Materialy*, p. 87.
74 Miliutina, 'Iz zapisok', *Russkaia Starina*, 98 (1899), p. 120.
75 Trubetskaia, *Materialy*, p. 129.
76 Bakhrushin, 'Velikaia Kniaginia Elena Pavlovna', p. 168.

Chapter 3

PRINCESS ISABEL AND THE ABOLITION OF SLAVERY

> Yesterday I had my first cabinet meeting, but first I should say to you that when Daddy left it seemed to me so strange to see myself a type of emperor from head to toe without changing my skin, without a beard and without a very fat belly.
>
> –Letter from Princess Isabel to D. Pedro II 4 June 1871[1]

> My statement about the loss of moral force and my insistence on the dismissal of the Chief-of-police resulted in the fall of the ministry. I don't regret what I did. Sooner or later, I would have done it. A silent anger possessed me and in conscience I could not continue with a Ministry when I felt and was convinced that it did not fulfil the aspirations of the country in the actual circumstances. God help me, and that the question of emancipation will shortly come to the last step that I so much want to see.
>
> –Letter from Princess Isabel to D. Pedro II 14 March 1888[2]

The seventeen years separating these two letters to her father marked Isabel's transition from a nervous young woman to an empress-in-waiting. The diffidence, hesitation and anxiety evident in 1871 had been replaced by conviction, determination and confidence by 1888. Above all, the exercise of power had become intrinsic to Isabel. Isabel began her first regency in 1871 as a political ingénue and ended her third regency in 1888 as an empress-in-waiting. It had been no easy matter for Isabel to reconcile her roles as a woman and as empress-to-be since they existed in constant tension with each other. As a woman Isabel was expected to subordinate herself to her father, her husband and finally her adult sons. As empress she would be the embodiment of the nation, the head of state and the focal point of the political system.

1 Arquivo Grão Para XLI-3-33-16 *Carta da Princesa Isabel a D. Pedro II 4 de junho 1871.*

2 Arquivo Grão Pará XLI-3-33 *Carta da Princesa Isabel a D. Pedro II 14 de março 1888.*

Isabel had to learn to manage these contradictory expectations, moving between them, emphasizing one and then the other at different stages of her life. Neither ever completely disappeared at any point, but as her life progressed Isabel increasingly adopted the mantle of empress-to-be. The three times she acted as regent for her father were critical stages in her shift away from her private role to her public one. This process reached its apogee during Isabel's third regency, when she decisively embraced her role as empress-to-be, placing herself at the head of the emancipation movement.

Early Life

Princess Isabel was born in 1846, the second of four children of Emperor Dom Pedro II and Empress Teresa Cristina. Isabel was not expected to inherit the throne as her two brothers had priority over her. However, both brothers were dead by 1850, leaving Isabel as the heir to the throne and completely changing the trajectory of her life. Princess Isabel's early life was one of stultifying stability, in marked contrast to Elena's chaotic and peripatetic childhood. The Emperor Dom Pedro II dominated the lives of his daughters and influenced their characters more than anyone else. He devised a rigorous educational program for them and often took the lessons himself. The girls' mother, Empress Teresa Cristina, was a secondary figure in the lives of the Isabel and Leopoldinha. Only in passing on her devout Catholicism to Isabel and her sister did the empress leave a lasting impression.[3]

The woman who was to exercise the most profound influence on Isabel was the Countess Barral, appointed by Dom Pedro to supervise the upbringing of his daughters. Her task laid down by the emperor was to ensure that 'the character of each of the princesses must be educated in a way that will be appropriate for women who are to direct a constitutional government of an Empire like that of Brazil'.[4] Barral was exceptionally well-qualified to achieve this goal. Intelligent, charming and beautiful, she had spent many years at the court of King Louis-Philippe in France, acquiring a degree of sophistication and poise that left men in awe of her, including the emperor.[5] She was also strong-willed and determined. Rejecting slavery as immoral she had freed her own slaves long before it was fashionable to do so. Far more than the empress who was the embodiment of the self-effacing woman, Barrel provided Isabel and her sister with a model of a woman that successfully combined power and agency with outward conformity to the demands of

3 Mesquita, *O Terceiro Reinado*, p. 23.

4 Carvalho, *D. Pedro II*, p. 66.

5 Del Priore *O Castelo*, p. 49.

a patriarchal society. Barral made Isabel aware of her of public role as heir, drumming into her that all her words and deeds, no matter how seemingly insignificant, were important and even her private utterances and actions had consequences in the public sphere.[6] It was a lesson Isabel did not forget. Until her death in 1891, Barral remained a friend and advisor to Isabel.

At fourteen, Isabel swore the oath of the allegiance demanded of the heir in a lavish ceremony before Parliament: 'I swear to maintain the Roman Catholic Apostolic religion, to comply with the political Constitution of the Brazilian nation and to be obedient to the laws and to the emperor'.[7] The dissonance between the expectations placed on Isabel as a woman and on Isabel as empress-to-be was profound and deeply disturbing for Isabel herself, her family and the wider society. It became more acute when Isabel became heir to the throne. On taking the oath Isabel passed from the private to the public sphere, required to enact the role of heir. From that moment every aspect of her life, even the most intimate, was a matter of public scrutiny and debate.

Father: Emperor Dom Pedro II

In many respects, Isabel conformed to the societal expectations of submission to male authority. Her father was a powerful presence in her life until his death in 1891. Isabel remained extremely close to him, expressing her affection for him in a manner which continually emphasized her role as a daughter and his as a father. Her love and respect for him were deeply rooted and did not diminish with the passage of the years. Isabel complied with the societal demands that emphasized male authority and female subordination. However, while the form remained unchanged, the substance of their relationship did not. As she grew older, Isabel subtly, but unmistakably, asserted herself and her opinions in opposition to her father when she felt her core beliefs were challenged.

Many historians have remarked that Dom Pedro, like most of the male elite, found the idea of rule by a woman deeply troubling and never really believed that Isabel would succeed him as empress.[8] His exclusion of Isabel from any participation in government and his refusal to discuss affairs of state with her even after her regencies is often cited as evidence of his lack of faith in Isabel ruling after his death.[9] Seen in isolation Dom Pedro's actions would seem to confirm this. However, in the context of the history of monarchy, there

6 Del Priore , *O Castelo de Papel*, p. 49.
7 Del Priore, O Castelo *de Papel*, p. 50.
8 Barman, *Citizen Emperor*, p. 129. Del Priore, *O Castelo de Papel*, p. 46.
9 Barman, *Citizen Emperor*, p. 287.

is nothing unusual about this. European monarchs often had deeply ambiguous feelings about their offspring succeeding them, desiring this, yet convinced that he or she lacked the requisite qualities. Queen Victoria, Dom Pedro's contemporary, had a very low opinion of Edward the Prince of Wales' abilities and resolutely excluded him from official roles for forty years, lamenting publicly 'Oh! What will become of the poor country when I die'.[10] Dom Pedro's behaviour towards his daughter expressed, by the standards of other monarchs, a large degree of confidence in her. In contrast to Victoria, Dom Pedro never publicly voiced doubts about his daughter's fitness to succeed. Rather than making inferences from what Dom Pedro did not do, it is far more instructive to look at what he did to ensure his daughter would succeed him.

Dom Pedro had insisted to Countess Barral that the education of Isabel (and her sister in case of Isabel's death) prepared her not only intellectually, but psychologically and morally for the role of empress. The emperor also sought a marriage partner for her that would raise the prestige of Isabel, the monarchy and Brazil. Above all, it is hard to square Dom Pedro's supposed lack of belief in his daughter with his extraordinary decision to make her regent while he took extended absences from his duties. On three separate occasions Dom Pedro handed over the reins of government to his daughter for a total of nearly four years: twice to go travelling and once because of illness. Of his contemporaries only Emperor Nicholas I of Russia had acted similarly, and for much briefer periods.[11] Some of Dom Pedro's advisors and many in Parliament wanted Isabel to have a purely ceremonial role without the powers of the emperor granted to her under the constitution while she was regent. Dom Pedro flatly rejected these proposals and insisted that Isabel have the full panoply of powers accorded to the emperor under the constitution.[12] On 17 May 1871, Parliament passed a bill authorizing the absence of the emperor, adding 'During the absence of H.M the Emperor Sra D. Isabel will govern in his place, as regent, with all the attributions which belong to the *Poder Moderador* and to the head of the Executive Power'.[13] None of this testifies to a lack of confidence in his daughter's capacities as empress.

After her marriage to the Conde d'Eu, grandson of Louis-Philippe of France (1830–1848), Dom Pedro continued to prepare Isabel for her future role. He sent Isabel to Europe with her husband to give her experience of the world beyond Brazil. Isabel's travels in Europe gave her the chance to meet other European monarchs, including Queen Victoria, and leading

10 P. Bartley, *Queen Victoria* (Abingdon, Oxon 2016), p. 179.

11 Tatishchev, *Imperator Aleksandr II*, vol. I. pp. 117–18.

12 Daibert, *Isabel*, p. 68.

13 Viana Lyra, 'Isabel de Bragança', pp. 106–112.

figures of Europe's political elites. Isabel was expected to see what a modern European state looked like and what Brazil should aspire to. In England, for example, as well as Queen Victoria, Isabel met with members of the elite and visited Parliament as she mentioned in her letter to her father in 1865.

> After this factory visit we went to the House of Parliament where we watched briefly a session of the House of Commons. The president [speaker] has a grey wig which gives him the appearance of rabbit with short ears. At night we went to a ball that the Prince of Wales gave to celebrate the second anniversary of his wedding, and to which he invited us and where we saw Lord Palmerston, Lord Granville etc.[14]

On her next visit to Europe in 1871, Isabel visited France in the aftermath of defeat in the Franco-Prussian War and was in Paris during the first days of the revolt of the Paris Commune. In a hurried note to her father she wrote on 20 March 'We saw Paris! my journal will tell you the rest when I bring it. I am saying this to you only so that you know we have left because of the revolution that was starting'[15] No less than her formal education, these travels provided Isabel with understanding of the world and her future role in it.

Husband: Conde d'Eu Gaston d'Orléans

Isabel's marriage, like all royal marriages, was a business arrangement. An alliance with the House of Orléans was seen as advantageous, connecting Isabel with the former ruling house of France and emphasizing the European nature of the Brazilian monarchy. Her husband Gaston, was very much a man of his time and class, particularly regarding his expectations of his wife. Like Prince Albert with Queen Victoria, Gaston believed it was his duty as husband to guide and instruct his wife, while she was obliged to obey him.[16] In all of this Gaston was fulfilling his role as a man and a husband. However, his dominance over his wife depended on ignoring the massive elephant in the room: Isabel would be empress, but Gaston would only ever be her consort. Opponents of Isabel's accession to the throne argued that Isabel would always be subordinate to her husband and through her, he would rule Brazil. For them, it was impossible for Isabel not to obey her husband, who would act in the interests of France, not Brazil.[17]

---

14 Arquivo Grão Pará XLI 3-33 *Carta da Princesa Isabel a Dom Pedro II 22 de março1865.*

15 Arquivo Grão Pará XLI 3-16 *Carta da Princesa Isabel a Dom Pedro II 20 de março 1871.*

16 Del Priore, *O Castelo de Papel*, p. 85.

17 See, for example, Sobrinho, *Antonio da Silva da Jardim*, p. 63.

Gaston Conde d'Eu 1870
Christiano Júnior
Public Domain Wikimedia Commons

Despite her conformity to the demands of her time, Isabel's relationship with her husband was always more complicated than simple submission. Over the course of their marriage, the balance of power within it shifted to Isabel not simply because she was heir apparent, but because she was the stronger character. Her husband had commanded Brazilian forces in the last stage of the Paraguayan War but, despite acquitting himself well, returned to Brazil with his nerves and confidence shattered. From that point, he seemed to become more dependent on Isabel and her letters usually contained a litany of the various ailments from which Gaston was suffering.[18]

Isabel's relationship with the two most important men in her life conformed in outward respects to the subordination demanded of other women. Isabel, however, was not other women. She was the heir to the throne, educated and trained to be an empress. Her subordination to her father was always limited and conditional, never absolute. It lessened as she grew in confidence and maturity in relation to both personal and political matters. In a remarkably frank letter to her father on 22 March 1888 Isabel matter-of-factly described her visit to the local brothel to find an old friend, Alphonse Karr, who she had heard was in town. 'If you see this good old man tell him for my part

18 Barman, *Princess Isabel*, pp. 108–109.

that I also very much want to see him, that I even dared to go to the door of the brothel (*Maison Close*), but that he wasn't there'.[19] By this point, neither father nor husband were dictating to Isabel about appropriate behaviour in her personal life. In politics too, when her core beliefs were challenged, Isabel showed a resoluteness of character and determination that belied the outward appearance of dutiful daughter and wife.

Isabel's Political Activity Outside of the Regencies

Dom Pedro, as we have seen, excluded Isabel from participation in government before her regencies and in the periods between them. She had few opportunities to show initiative or take part in any political activity. Given the restricted environment within which she was confined, this was not surprising. Many historians have commented on the seeming absence of any political interest in the affairs of the empire, concluding that she was an essentially apolitical woman.[20] This was not the case. Isabel understood the delicacy of her position as heir very well, further complicated of course because she was a woman. Father and husband both guarded the boundaries of Isabel's activity. Nevertheless, in spite of the gendered role assigned to her and nearly always respected by her, Isabel did directly intervene in the political process when her core beliefs were challenged. The first time this happened was in the 1860s over the conflict between Church and State and the second time in 1886 to thwart the intention of Prime Minister Cotegipe to close the Quilombo of Leblon, a refuge for fugitive slaves.

Church and state in Brazil had existed relatively harmoniously until the papal interdiction on freemasonry in the 1860s.[21] The conflict escalated and led to the imprisonment of two Brazilian bishops who refused to ignore the papal command to exclude freemasons from the church. Dom Pedro firmly supported the government in this matter.[22] Isabel, however, equally firmly opposed the government line and her father.[23] She was appalled by the arrest of the bishops.[24] According to the demands of her time, whatever degree of anger she felt over the arrest of the bishops, Isabel should have kept

19 Arquivo de Grão Pará II XLI.3.33 *Carta da Princesa Isabel a D.Pedro 22 de março 1888.*

20 Barman, *Princess Isabel*, p. 96, Del Priore, *O Castelo de Papel*, pp. 73–74.

21 Carvalho, *Dom Pedro II*, pp. 152–153.

22 Barman, *Citizen Emperor*, p. 248. Carvalho, *Dom Pedro II*, p. 154.

23 Carvalho, *Dom Pedro II*, p. 156.

24 L.L. Lacombe *Isabel A Princesa Redentora: Biografia baseada em Documentos inéditos* (Petrópolis, 1989), p. 202.

her feelings to herself. In opposing the arrest, Isabel confronted a solid phalanx of male authority including her father. This was one of the few occasions on which the political elite was united across party lines. For a woman to speak out in these circumstances required considerable courage and conviction. This conflict rumbled on yet Isabel remained steadfast in her opposition to the government line, writing to her father to express her displeasure:

> My dear and good little daddy
> Your letters always give me so much pleasure! Write to me whenever you can. The business with the bishops also worries me a lot. Could they have been more prudent? What I think is that the government also wants to interfere in things that should not be within its reach. Apart from this if the masons have such an attachment to matters of the church that they do not want to be expelled from it why don't they abandon masonry? Or is there fear or a little lack of fervour on their side? We must defend the rights of the citizen and of the Constitution, but what security is there in all this for which oaths were sworn if in the first place we do not obey the Church![25]

While recognizing that the bishops could have been more tactful, Isabel defended the Church, arguing that the state had no right to interfere in an internal church matter. This placed her squarely in opposition to the prevailing political consensus – an entirely male consensus of course. Isabel's voice in this letter is neither timid nor deferential, but brusque and businesslike. Neither was this a trivial question for which the borders of gender spheres could be fudged. It was one of the great questions of state, not just in Brazil but in many states in South America and beyond. Isabel transgressed that boundary boldly and deliberately. This was not just a private matter between Isabel and her father. Isabel's opposition to the imprisonment of the bishops was widely known and attracted condemnation in the press and among politicians who were outraged at Isabel's interference in a political matter.[26] A woman with political opinions of her own and a readiness to voice it was a direct challenge to the prevailing norms of gender behaviour.

The second occasion when Isabel intervened was during the political crisis brought about by the anti-slavery campaign. Flatly contradicting those historians who argue Isabel was a very late convert to the anti-slavery cause, joining it only in the last few weeks before emancipation, Isabel's

---

25 O Arquivo Grão Pará XLI 3-33 *Carta da Princesa Isabel a Dom Pedro II 31 de augusto 1873.*
26 Priore, *O Papel de Castelo*, pp. 152–154. The masons in particular detested Isabel.

actions again tally with her belief only to act when one of her core principles was threatened and then as discreetly as possible. Isabel moved to counter a direct threat to one of the most important symbols of the anti-slavery movement, the *Quilombo* of Leblon. This refuge for fugitive slaves, positioned very close to the capital, was an affront to Prime Minister Cotegipe and he sought the emperor's permission to forcefully close it down. However, Isabel prevailed upon her father to reject Cotegipe's request, something the prime minister neither forgave nor forgot.[27] Isabel's sparing use of her authority as heir-to-be did not signify a lack of interest in politics or current affairs, but was a product of her training and her own understanding of her constitutional role and her role as a woman. Managing those roles was a delicate business. In Isabel's understanding, this did not preclude intervention but limited it only to the most serious challenges to Isabel's beliefs and values. The attack on the Church and the attempt to shut down one of the most powerful symbols of the anti-slavery movement justified Isabel's direct intervention, in her own eyes at least.

Paraguayan War 1864–1870

The Paraguayan War was one of the bloodiest and least known of all nineteenth-century conflicts. A rumbling dispute over the Rio de la Plata region exploded into the bloodiest war in South American history. On one side were Brazil, Argentina and Uruguay and on the other Paraguay. Despite the vast imbalance in resources, the war dragged on for more than six years. The impact of the war on Brazil was profound immediately and in the longer term. It brought the popularity of the emperor to its peak, created an army in Brazil where none had existed before and subtly altered the balance of power between the rural areas and the urban ones in favour of the latter.[28] As far as slavery was concerned, the war indirectly opened the path to abolition. The recruitment of slaves into the army in return for their freedom raised awkward questions about citizenship and patriotism. Isabel's husband, who became commander-in-chief of the Brazilian army in the latter stages of the war unilaterally freed all the slaves in Paraguay, a decision which astonished and annoyed the slave-owning classes in Brazil in equal measure.[29] Most importantly, the war provided the platform for the emperor to raise the issue of abolition directly and publicly.

---

27 Silva *As Camélias do Leblon*, p. 26; Lacombe, *A Princesa Redentora*, p. 224.
28 Carvalho, *Dom Pedro II*, p. 126.
29 Mesquita, *O Terceiro Reinado*, p. 37.

In his speech from the throne at the opening of Parliament on 22 May 1867 Dom Pedro unexpectedly raised the issue of emancipation.

> The servile element in the Empire cannot fail to merit your timely consideration, taking action in such a way that while respecting existing property rights and without profoundly disrupting our first industry – agriculture, the high concerns regarding emancipation can be attended to.[30]

The words were even more opaque and oblique than Alexander's to the Moscow nobility a decade earlier, but those listening to or reading them were under no doubt about what they meant. The emperor had placed emancipation firmly on the agenda. The speech was an assertion of monarchical power, springing from Dom Pedro's own beliefs about emancipation. His prestige and authority were at its peak, providing Dom Pedro with the opportunity to move for the first time openly towards emancipation.

Dom Pedro's efforts bore fruit four years later with the Law of the Free Womb. All children born into slavery after the passage of the law were to be freed on their 21st birthday. On its own, the law did nothing for those already slaves, but it did condemn slavery to a lingering death. Its real significance, however, lay in destroying the belief that slavery was an inalienable right and not subject to interference from the outside. The law was bitterly contested by the slave owners and it required all the accumulated prestige and authority of the emperor to get the bill passed into law.[31] Once it had completed all the parliamentary stages, Dom Pedro took his first extended trip abroad, leaving Isabel to sign the bill into law.

Isabel's First Regency 20 May 1871–31 March 1872

Isabel's letter to her father cited at the beginning of the chapter expressed in light-hearted but graphic terms the association of political power with maleness. A rough male skin, a beard and a fat belly, her father, in other words, emphasized that public power was intrinsic to men, and by implication abnormal for women. Isabel, however, now found herself forced to play a role for which she had been prepared, but which went against everything her society and her times believed about women.

For any heir, the first exercise of power and responsibility as head of state must have been a daunting undertaking, but for Isabel, lacking those

30 *Falas do Trono de Dom Pedro I, Dom Pedro II e Princesa Isabel* (Brasília, 2019), pp. 488–489.

31 Carvalho, *A Construção da Ordem*, pp. 311–312.

quintessential male traits, the alien nature of the enterprise was even more acute. However, if she had expected the experience to be an exercise in wielding the charismatic and legal powers of the emperor, she had rude awaking as she discovered that she was in effect the empire's first bureaucrat.

> When I entered into the room I was dismayed, five enormous folders stuffed full in monstrous manner were waiting for me. Fortunately, the matter was easier than I had thought at first sight. A great part of the pile of papers were letters for me to sign to the Sultan, the Emperor of Austria, etc etc. I don't know if also there was something for the Emperor of China as only by the address can you know to whom it is directed. There was also an infinity of Baronets, Viscounts etc etc for me to sign.[32]

Despite Isabel's shock and awkwardness in her new role, a propitious moment had been chosen for her first regency. The prestige and authority of the emperor was at its peak. He had just led the country through the gruelling and very costly war against Paraguay from which it had emerged victorious. With the war over, the empire was stable and appeared to on the verge of significant political and economic reforms.

Isabel's regency began after the bill had passed all its parliamentary stages but still required the imperial signature to become law. Dom Pedro, however, deliberately chose to give Isabel the honour of signing the law, associating his daughter and heir indelibly with emancipation in the public mind.[33] Few monarchs would have passed up the chance to go down in history as one of the great liberators of humanity, even in favour of their own offspring. Dom Pedro's abnegation was an investment in the future of the monarchy and of Isabel. He laid the groundwork for Isabel to appear as a progressive, enlightened monarch guiding the country to its place among the civilized nations, above all Europe. Isabel duly signed the Law of the Free Womb to great public rejoicing and acclaim. Isabel's popularity soared in consequence of signing the law.[34] The image of Isabel '*a Redentora*', the Redeemer, was already under construction.

Isabel's first regency passed without controversy. She fulfilled her functions to general approval. In terms of a political experiment, it had been a success. She had gained valuable experience of what it meant to be head of state, had won general approval and had begun the process of accustoming the Brazilian elite to a woman as ruler. However, conditions had been very favourable for

32 Arquivo Grão Pará XLI 3.16 *Carta da Princesa Isabel a Dom Pedro II 4 de junho 1871.*
33 Daibert, *Isabel*, p. 69.
34 Schwarcz, *As Barbas*, p. 315.

Isabel, who had been carefully chaperoned by senior ministers, bureaucrats and her husband. Her room for independent activity in her first regency had been practically non-existent.

Isabel's Second Regency 26 March 1876–27 September 1877

Isabel became regent for the second time in 1876 when her father took another extended vacation. For Isabel, this was a dismal time in which she was subjected to levels of abuse and criticism for which there was no precedent. Brazilian society was becoming more urbanized, less deferential and increasingly impatient at what appeared to be the slow rate of development in the country. The emperor, in particular, became a target of ridicule, frequently referred to as Dom Pedro Banana, not the most flattering epithet for a monarch.[35] Inklings of these profound changes in Brazilian society had already been present during Isabel's first regency, but they were barely discernible. By 1876 they burst upon Isabel with a ferocity that was deeply shocking and wounding. The goodwill towards the emperor which had muted criticism in the past was diminishing in the wake of these changes and the deep fear of being ruled by a woman was given voice by the press and political class in a way that would have no precedent until the tabloid press of the late twentieth century.[36]

Isabel, as regent and as a thirty-year-old woman, now became the lightning rod for all these fears and angers.[37] She was attacked relentlessly for being a woman, for marrying a foreigner and for not tackling Brazil's deep-rooted structural problems. In all of this criticism, Isabel had to remain silent as required by her role as regent. In addition, she was also pregnant again which unleashed a new wave of criticism against her. Pregnancy was further proof of Isabel's unfitness to govern.[38]

Unlike her first regency where the empire was still basking in the glow of military victory, the mood in the country was much grimmer. First, a serious drought began in the northeast, the intensity and duration of which brought misery on a vast scale to the region.[39] Second, blame for the electoral fraud and violence, which were permanent features of Brazilian democracy, was laid at the door of the emperor and by extension Isabel. Finally, the church/state conflict continued to rumble on. Isabel was of course already deeply

35 Schwarcz, *As Barbas*, p. 416.
36 Barman, *Princess Isabel*, p. 147.
37 Del Priore, *Castelo de Papel*, p. 162.
38 Barman, *Princess Isabel*, p. 150.
39 Del Priore *O Castelo de Papel*, pp. 162–164; Barman, *Princess Isabel*, p. 143.

compromised in the eyes of the male establishment for her support of the church. The appointment of a new papal nuncio again revived the conflict as Isabel told her father:

> From the newspapers you will see the commotion which has been caused by the news of the arrival of a new papal nuncio: a nuncio like any other. I don't believe, however, that it is anything other than nonsense.[40]

None of these problems could be solved by Isabel as regent. The role of the emperor was not to intervene in the day-to-day running of the country which was the government's responsibility. Electoral violence and fraud were at the heart of Brazilian democracy, enabling the great slave owners to control the political system.[41] The emperor had not been able to solve this problem in over thirty years of rule; Isabel exercising a temporary regency could do nothing.

Isabel's letters to her father at this time almost never touched on political matters. But in a letter in April 1876 Isabel, in a rare moment of openness, spoke of the few joys of power and also of her ambitions for the empire in the future.

> We have finished the Church holiday. I pardoned six convicts and commuted 2 death penalties. It is one of the only attributes of power that I like. I would also like the power to push improvements in the country, railways, colonisation etc etc but the wagon is heavy, and I don't know if I will have the strength to help in what way may be possible.[42]

Railways and colonization were seen as essential to modernizing Brazil. Colonization was internal, not surprising given the enormous size of Brazil. But it also hinted at land reform, a theme that would become more persistent and was almost as fraught as the issue of slavery.

Isabel's dismal experience during her second regency exposed her to the changed political conditions within the empire. She and her family had been subjected to levels of criticism that were wounding beyond measure. At the same time, she had received important lessons in the limitations of power and the frustrations inherent in her position as regent. Confronting long-term, almost insoluble problems such as political fraud and drought offered little chance for Isabel to intervene. Nevertheless, it is clear that Isabel had a vision for the empire's future and her role in it. Isabel's own words indicate that already at this point she did not see herself as passive tool of the elite

---

40 Arquivo Grão Pará XLI.3.21 *Carta da Princesa Isabel a Dom Pedro II 7 de augusto 1876.*

41 R. Graham, *Patronage and Politics in Nineteenth Century Brazil* (Stanford, 1990) p. 78.

42 *Aquivo Grão Pará XLI.31.21 Carta da Princesa Isabel a Dom Pedro II* 14 de abril 1876.

men around her, but was starting to conceive of herself as empress, leading the empire. That she was daunted by the scale of the task is hardly to be wondered at. Painful as the second regency had been for Isabel, it had been a valuable apprenticeship for rule.

Saraiva Law 1885

The momentum that had driven the emancipation process from the emperor's speech in 1867 came to an end with the passage of the Law of the Free Womb in 1871. The emperor seemed unwilling to confront the slavery lobby head-on again and, until the closing years of the decade, the issue went into abeyance. However, by the late 1870s a genuine anti-slavery movement had at last appeared in Brazil. Beginning from the ground up in Ceara state in the northeast of Brazil, the movement sought to end slavery province by province across Brazil. Mobilizing vast numbers of people, especially women, the anti-slavery campaign engaged large sections of Brazilian society. Masters were pressured or persuaded to free their slaves or funds were raised to purchase slaves whose masters refused. Province after province was cleared of slavery in this manner.[43] Despite the great success of this movement, it ran up against two intractable problems. Firstly, the movement had very little traction in the three states where slaves were overwhelmingly concentrated: São Paulo, Rio de Janeiro and Minas Gerais. Secondly, declaring provinces free of slavery did not abolish slavery. Slavery was protected under the constitution and only imperial law could change this.

This movement did, however, galvanize the government to make a new effort to reform slavery. It could hardly be described as bold, freeing all slaves over sixty. Yet it did not make it through Parliament. Instead, a new government piloted through Parliament a watered-down version of the law. Slaves were to be freed at sixty, but would have to work for a further three years to compensate their masters. The law passed, but it fell far short of the expectations of the hopes for complete abolition. The effect of the law was to take the wind out of the sails of the anti-slavery movement, but the lull was only temporary. It was at this moment that Isabel's third regency began.

The Third Regency 28 June 1887–22 August 1888

Unlike her first two regencies, Isabel's third regency was unplanned. She and her family had just departed for Europe when they received a telegram informing them of the emperor's grave illness and orders for her immediate

---

43 Conrad, *The Destruction of Brazilian Slavery*, pp. 189–193.

return to Brazil. The situation in the country was alarming too. The anti-slavery campaign was mobilizing Brazilian society in a way not seen since the War of Independence nearly seventy years earlier.[44] Slaves began to abandon the plantations of Sao Paulo, seeking refuge in any number of havens or *quilombos*.[45] The final elimination of slavery in Brazil, however, depended on political decisions at the centre of power. The government, led by the Prime Minister, the Barão de Cotegipe, placed itself in direct opposition to this movement. Cotegipe, in command of stable parliamentary government and supported by his cabinet, resolutely rejected any further moves to abolition.[46] The threat of serious unrest grew as the government, backed by the slaveholding elites of Rio de Janeiro, Sao Paulo and Minas Gerais, the three great slave states in Brazil, determined to face down this movement.

Personally and politically, Isabel confronted very difficult circumstances. Her beloved father was gravely ill and was not expected to survive. Isabel described her shock on seeing him when she returned from Europe.

> There we found my father free of the crisis and fever that he had gone through, but still very thin and weak. But what I noticed most was a certain lack of memory in his robust intelligence that I was accustomed to know without the least flaw.[47]

Dom Pedro left for Europe almost immediately, but he remained in Isabel's thoughts throughout the next fifteen months. Politically, Isabel had to cope with the crisis caused by the abolition campaign and the refusal of the government to make any concessions. The Prime Minister the Barão de Cotegipe was an experienced, urbane politician who regarded the abolition movement, in spite of all its fury, as a temporary phenomenon that would soon burn itself out. He was determined that government policy would not be made in the streets and was unyielding in his determination to resist. As he put it in a debate in the Senate after his fall from power 'good governments are not guided by outbursts of public enthusiasm'.[48] He had other motives for resisting the public campaign for abolition. He rightly saw abolition not as the end of a process, but the start of a still more radical reconstruction of Brazilian society. In the same debate on the law in the Senate he warned of this.

44 Carvalho, *D. Pedro II*, pp. 190–191; Barman, *Princess Isabel*, pp. 170–171. H.S. Klein and F.V. Lima, *Slavery in Brazil* (Cambridge, 2010), pp. 308–310.

45 Conrad, *The Destruction of Brazilian Slavery*, p. 247.

46 Lacombe, *Isabel*, p. 225. Barman, *Princess Isabel*, p. 175.

47 Arquivo da Casa Imperial do Brasil *Maço* 199 – Doc 9030.

48 *Extinçao Da Escravidaão no Brasil. Discussao na Camara dos Deputados e no Senado* (Rio de Janeiro, Imprensa Nacional, 1889), p. 60.

> You know what are the consequences? It is not a secret. From here in a short while the division of lands and latifundia will be requested of which there are examples in many nations either for nothing or for a minimum price and then the state will decree the expropriation without compensation.[49]

Beneath his veneer of politeness, Cotegipe had contempt for Isabel.[50] In the absence of the emperor, he regarded himself as the ruler of the country as several satirical cartoons published at the time depicted.[51] On her side, Isabel, as the Constitution demanded was determined to work with him as she later recalled:

> Today the irritation caused by the Barão de Cotegipe at the beginning of the year has softened. He in his usual way has made me believe again that, though he was certainly wrong in his judgements and not acting in the best interests of the country, at least he was doing it in good faith and he wanted to serve me…
>
> The Barão de Cotegipe seemed able to handle the situation and I knew his firm inclinations to support everything in relation to religion, inclinations unfortunately rare. Furthermore, I don't like shocks unless I am convinced that they would have useful and certain results and there was no reason at that point that would make me think less of the ministry. I saw fit to keep the ministry and in this way, we lived harmoniously for a long time.[52]

Cotegipe knew Isabel's feelings regarding abolition and no doubt would have preferred to deal with an ailing, very ill old man rather than a young vigorous woman with strong opinions. Isabel at her first meeting with Cotegipe offered some mild criticism of the way her father's illness had been handled by the government. 'I told him that I found weakness in the ministry's procedure. To that he retorted that the life of my father would have been at risk if he hadn't acted so and with that he shut me up'.[53] The brusque manner in which her Prime Minister had dismissed her tentative suggestion set the tone for their subsequent relationship.

---

49 *Extincao da Escravidão no Brasil*, p. 68.

50 Del Priore, *O Castelo de Papel*, p. 207.

51 See, for example, *Revista Illustrada* 5 February 1887; Schwarcz, *As Barbas do Imperador*, p. 420.

52 Arquivo da Casa Imperial do Brasil Maço 199 – Doc 9030.

53 Arquivo da Casa Imperial do Brasil Maço 199 – Doc 9030.

Isabel at first believed that Cotegipe would eventually respond to both her own promptings and the crisis unfolding in the country. But whenever Isabel tried to raise the matter with Cotegipe he responded with a mixture of evasiveness and promises to look into the matter. Isabel grasped quickly that he had no intention of doing anything to solve the crisis. 'With each day that passed, I was more and more convinced he would do nothing'.[54] Isabel now faced a dilemma. According to the norms of the Constitution, she should accept the decision of the government and support it. She had voiced her opinion to the government, but it was not obliged to act on it. On the other hand, the clamour for decisive action to end slavery was becoming ever louder, and increasingly Isabel herself was becoming the focus of that criticism. The *Gazetta da Tarde*, an abolitionist newspaper, attacked Isabel's inaction in no uncertain terms.

> Her Highness, the Regent, does not believe that the preservation of the Barão de Cotegipe can do any harm to the country. The complaint of those who think that the retention for one more day of this cabinet of slavery, for slavery and by slavery is a shameful imposition on the nation must even seem impatiently disrespectful to Her Highness. Sooner or later there will be a reckoning not with the Barão of Cotegipe, who is only on leave from the grave and will return with other lost souls, but with those who supported him.[55]

Isabel's speech from the throne on the closing of Parliament on 15 October 1887 only compounded this impatience. She made no mention at all of slavery or abolition, reflecting the government's determination to resist the popular movement.[56] The *Revista Illustrada* pointed out the absurdity of Isabel's silence on this issue: 'As if her memory was suffering she forgot completely to mention the problem of slavery, that is the subject that in the highest degree is demanding the attention of the Brazilian people'.[57] Caught between the intransigence of the government and the abolition campaign in the country at large, Isabel was assailed from all sides.

By the end of 1887, Isabel's attempts to influence the government had failed. She had exhausted all options under the Constitution apart from the use of the *poder moderador* which justified the dismissal of the elected government

---

54 Arquivo da Casa Imperial do Brasil Maço 199 – Doc 9030.

55 *Gazeta da Tarde* 20 August 1887.

56 *Império Brasileiro:Falas do Trono desde o ano de 1823 até o ano de 1889* (Brasília, 1977), pp. 501–502.

57 *Revista Illustrada* 22 October 1887.

only 'in cases which the salvation of the state demands it'.[58] Its use in these circumstances, however, would be unprecedented and most likely would unleash another political crisis. As in her second regency, Isabel's desires ran up against the constitutional limitations of her position. To assert herself in this situation would have defied convention in terms of the Constitution and the patriarchal ideology of the time. Assertion required a conscious decision by Isabel to attempt to impose her will on the flow of political events. Her repeated attempts over the course of several months to prod Cotegipe into action belie the depiction of her actions as hurried, spontaneous or ill-thought out.

> The question of abolition was going forward, its ideas were winning me over more and more each day and there were no publications in relation to it that I didn't read. I am even more convinced that it was necessary to do something in this matter.[...] Meanwhile Sr Barão promised to study the question. With each day that passed I was more and more convinced that he would do nothing.[59]

Restricted formally by the Constitution, Isabel drew on another resource of monarchical power, its charisma. Isabel began receiving camellias every day – a banal act, but one that was charged with political significance. The white camelia had become the symbol of all those committed to a radical abolition. Isabel was sending an unmistakable political message to the country about emancipation by receiving and wearing camellias. But the message was still more explicit because the camellias came from the *Quilombo* of Leblon just outside Rio de Janeiro, the very one that Isabel had prevented Cotegipe from closing before her third regency. They were grown by fugitive slaves who had found shelter there. Isabel's actions aroused widespread comment in the press as she had intended and as she knew from her governess' teaching, all her actions had significance.[60] For the Cabinet to function, it had to possess the confidence of the emperor and be seen to enjoy it.[61] Isabel thus began the process of undermining the government without formally stepping outside the powers granted to her by the Constitution. It is hard to equate Isabel's choice not just of camellias, already the symbol of radical abolition, but camellias from Leblon with a supposed commitment to abolition in its most conservative form.

---

58 O. Nogueira (ed) *Constituiçoes Brasileiras* (3rd ed, Brasília, 2012), p. 76.
59 Arquivo da Casa Imperial do Brasil *Maço* 199 – Doc 9030.
60 Silva, *As Camélias do Leblon*, p. 35.
61 Needle, *The Party of Order*, p. 230.

Isabel's actions became bolder and more radical She allowed the summer palace at Petrópolis to give shelter to fugitive slaves.[62] Neither Alexander II nor Abraham Lincoln ever opened the Winter Palace or the White House to fugitive serfs or slaves. Isabel permitted her two young children to edit a pro-abolitionist newspaper which came out twice a week, *O Imperial Corrense*.[63] Despite nominally being the work of the children, Isabel was of course the editor and it was her anti-slavery opinions that were published, as everybody understood. These were extraordinary acts for the head of a slave state to take and represented an unmistakable political declaration of her own views on abolition. By these actions, Isabel broke decisively with the passive role that was allotted to her as a woman, even a woman who was regent. They were acts of calculated risk for herself and for the monarchy. Through them, Isabel was defining a new role for herself and for the monarchy, stretching its powers and publicly realigning it with different sections of Brazilian society and irrevocably breaking with its former supporters, the slaveholders. It is hard to see these actions as conservative, timid or just simply reactive as they have frequently been portrayed. Isabel's public identification with the most radical section of the abolitionist movement was on the contrary bold and unprecedented, even more so because she was a woman.

Isabel's political activism moved from symbolic actions to direct interventions into the political process. She increased her pressure in her private meetings with Cotegipe, warning him that the government would fall if he did not act.

> Again I called the attention of the Barão de Cotegipe to the question and the strength that the ministry was losing everywhere. I only just refrained from telling him that he should retire (the cup was beginning to overflow.) But the Barão seemed to understand nothing and with his many fine words and great skill he was still more cunning than me.[64]

A clear indication of the breakdown of trust was that Isabel suspected that Cotegipe was not informing the Cabinet of their conversations so she repeated her warning in front of the entire cabinet.

> Days later in a ministerial meeting I thought I should repeat in front of all the ministers (fearing that the Sr Barão would keep his ideas only for

62 Daibert, *Isabel*, p. 129.
63 Del Priore, *O Castelo de Papel*, p. 218.
64 Arquivo da Casa Imperial do Brasil *Maço* 199 – Doc 9030.

> me) what was said in private. I added to what I had written what I had also said to Sr Barão, namely that the Ministry could not continue if they did nothing if favour of emancipation and that it would be an evil for the Conservative party.[65]

It could not have been easy for Isabel as woman to deliver such an ultimatum to men at the pinnacle of the political establishment, but it marked the distance Isabel had travelled from her first Cabinet meeting in 1871 and her sense of awkwardness in fulfilling her imperial role. She was now wielding power with determination and using her intelligence to guide her use of that power and avoid playing into Cotegipe's hands.

As often in a major political crisis, a relatively trivial incident broke the deadlock. The Rio de Janeiro police badly beat up an anti-slavery activist, which in itself was hardly newsworthy. However, it suddenly became an issue of great public controversy. Isabel found in this incident a way out of the political impasse. She insisted that those responsible be disciplined. Cotegipe was willing to fire the local police chief, but Isabel insisted that the head of the police in the city take responsibility. Isabel was now behaving as no woman had ever done in history of the Brazilian state. She was dictating the terms on which she would allow the government to continue. Cotegipe rightly saw this as the complete withdrawal of confidence in his government and offered his resignation which Isabel accepted.[66] The fall of the Ministry opened the way for a new one, committed to abolition.

Isabel informed her father of what had happened in a letter, part of which forms the epigraph at the beginning of the chapter. The events that Isabel describes are remarkable enough, but what is more surprising is the tone of this letter to her father.

> About the ministry you have known what happened from the newspapers. For some time now my ideas have diverged from those of the Ministry. I felt that the government had lost a lot of moral force. I had already said something like this a few weeks ago, now with more firmness and in writing, reproaching at the same time for the most part the police authorities for what had happened. Or rather the attitudes taken by the police authorities which has been going on for a long time. My statement about the loss of moral force and my insistence on the dismissal of the Chief of police resulted in the fall of the ministry.[67]

---

65 Arquivo da Casa Imperial do Brasil *Maço* 199 – Doc 9030.

66 Arquivo da Casa Imperial do Brasil *Maço* 199 – Doc 9030.

67 Arquivo de Grão Pará XLI 33 *Carta da Princesa Isabel a Dom Pedro II 14 de março1888.*

It is already the tone of a woman accustomed to the wielding of power and accepting responsibility for her decisions. Isabel did not seek her father's advice before dismissing the Ministry, nor seek his approval after the fact. She acted on her own authority and according to her own lights. In her testament, Isabel regretted only that she had not acted sooner. 'I was ashamed of myself that by an excess of indolence in avoiding conflict which is always disagreeable to me, I didn't force the Ministry to resign as soon as I felt that it was not good for the country and was dragging me to the abyss with it.'[68]

Isabel was developing an acute set of political antennae, seeking to anticipate political problems before they arose. Cotegipe suggested to Isabel that they delay the announcement of the resignation of the government until the opening of Parliament when the government could issue a statement making clear that it could do nothing more regarding emancipation and warning Isabel that precipitous action might endanger the crown. Isabel, however, was by now deeply wary of Cotegipe and feared he could be laying a trap for her.

> Would it have been better to let things continue until the opening of the Chambers, bearing in mind the obstacles raised by the Ministry, and then being obliged to ask for the resignation of the Ministry? I don't think so. I don't know how the country could have endured the 2 months that remained and apart from this I was totally aware of the traditional manner of Sr Barão de Cotegipe. I am not afraid to confess it – I feared that yet again he would ensnare me and I would not be able to strike in the way I judged necessary.[69]

Isabel refused Cotegipe's request and, in a clear assertion of her growing control over the political process, rejected his nomination of a successor and selected her own, Sr João Alfredo another conservative but one whom she knew was committed to abolition. 'As for the choice of the new ministers it was me who indicated João Alfredo. He chose the other ones. I gave him complete freedom to organized the cabinet as was necessary in view of the parliamentary majority'.[70]

Isabel, however, did not leave João Alfredo completely free to carry out abolition. She insisted that the abolition must be immediate and without compensation. The latter in particular aroused the fury of the slave owners

68 *Arquivo da Casa Imperial do Brasil* Maço 199 – Doc 9030.

69 *Arquivo da Casa Imperial do Brasil Maço* 199 – Doc 9030.

70 Arquivo de Grão Pará *II XLI.3.33 Carta da Princesa Isabel a Dom Pedro 14 de março 1888.*

who had been counting on generous compensation. Isabel dismissed any attempt at compensation on the grounds that it was immoral and the country had no money. Again this was an extraordinary intervention on the part of Isabel which effectively deprived the slave owners of their ability to manipulate the emancipation legislation to their advantage.

> And indemnities? Although on that matter I had never expressed my opinion before the project had been formulated I could not accept it as appropriate or fair. Certain scruples could have affected me, but I dismissed them.[...] Besides this as I have already said, the idea of the injustice of slavery and the long time that the lords exploited their slaves could not fail to act on my spirit.[71]

After the appointment of João Alfredo, the emancipation bill passed its parliamentary stages in record time, ready for Isabel to sign on 13 May 1888. The Act was both extraordinarily laconic and extraordinarily unambiguous.

> The Regent Princess Imperial, in the name of His Majesty the Emperor, Sr Dom Pedro II, makes known to all the subjects of the Empire that the General Assembly has decreed and She has sanctioned the following Law:
>
> Art.1. Slavery is declared extinct in Brazil from the date of this Law.
>
> Art.2. All articles to the contrary are revoked.[72]

Isabel had arrived at the point where she now was the focus of political power in the country. She had dismissed one cabinet, appointed another in defiance of accepted convention and gave clear instructions about what she expected from this cabinet which duly complied with them. In addition, Isabel's authority was immeasurably increased by the public adulation of her that swept the country. Isabel's opponents, far from seeing her as passive tool of other forces, denounced her for carrying out a coup. In the Senate, an opponent of abolition accused Isablel of being responsible for 'a measure which in conception and scope is frankly revolutionary'.[73] Already she was referred to as '*a Redentora*', the Redeemer, a title with unmistakable references to Christ. She was spoken of no longer as the Princesa Imperial, but simply Isabel I. In the aftermath of emancipation, Isabel held unparalleled authority in her hands.

---

71 Arquivo da Casa Imperial do Brasil Maço 199 – Doc 9030.

72 https://www2.senado.leg.br/bdsf/item/id/385454.

73 *Extinção da Escravidão*, p. 74.

Conclusion

By the end of her third regency, Isabel had indeed come 'to see herself a type of emperor from head to toe'. The young, rather awkward regent of 1871 had become an empress-in-waiting by 1888. Her demeanour, her authority and above all her self-belief had been transformed in the intervening years. Any heir to a throne had to make this transition, but for a woman of that era and that society it was particularly difficult. The constraints which had bound her in 1871 of upbringing, ideology and her constitutional role continued to apply in 1887–1888. Isabel, however, had changed. She had learnt that those constraints, while powerful, did not reduce her to the level of a passive observer of events. Her role as regent gave her the opportunity to take part in the political process and indeed to shape it to achieve her own ends. She did that using her constitutional powers, even at times barely remaining within the bounds of accepted practice. The use of these powers required intelligence, determination and courage, none of which Isabel lacked. The third regency provided a cause, the abolition of slavery, and a context, the anti-slavery movement, for Isabel to act in a way that neither of her first two regencies had done. But a cause was not a plan of action, a set of goals or a means to achieve them. These required the active intervention of Isabel which began when she realized Cotegipe, far from sharing her desire to achieve emancipation, actively sought to block it. Isabel's actions were not spontaneous, naïve or hurried. They were a product of rational calculation, careful preparation and a willingness to seize an opportunity when it finally arose. Nor did Isabel opt for the least radical outcome. She identified herself with the radical wing of abolitionism before the signing of the abolition act and insisted that it was immediate and uncompensated. All of this belies the standard portrait of Isabel as marionette of the men around her or the circumstances she found herself in. By the end of her third regency, Isabel was in truth an empress-to-be, not simply in the sense that her father's life was coming to an end and that she was next in line to throne, but that she had embraced her role as head of state, pillar of the constitution and wielder of the *poder moderador.*

In 1946 the *Revista do Instituto Histórico e Geográfico Brasileiro*, Brazil's leading historical journal, published a special edition to mark the centenary of Isabel's birth. In it, Carolina Nabuco, daughter of Joaquim Nabuco, summarized Isabel's contribution to the abolition of slavery

> Dona Isabel provoked and accepted the resignation of an anti-abolitionist ministry and replaced it with one favourable to Abolition. This obviously entailed a risk, as well as being an initiative that was not

> properly the Crown's responsibility, but rather that of Parliament. She was thus almost exclusively responsible for the Abolition of Slavery at that moment: that is in a vastly more rapid and much more complete manner than would have been possible in any other circumstances.[74]

There may be some element of hyperbole here, but it is a fitting epitaph for Isabel's contribution to the freeing of the slaves.

74 C. Nabuco 'A Redentora e os Abolicionistas', *Revista do Instituto Histórico e Geográfico Brasileiro*, 192 (1946), p. 89.

CONCLUSION

Emancipation had been a triumph for both Elena and Isabel. Servile labour was definitively ended in the two empires, in itself an epochal achievement. However, the issues of inclusion, citizenship and equality raised by emancipation were not resolved. In the Russian Empire, peasants remained alienated by the terms of emancipation and were never reconciled to the loss of land and the payment of redemption fees. They remained second-class citizens until the 1905 Revolution. Twelve years later, the peasants finally received the land settlement they had always wanted, taking all the land and expelling forever the remnants of their former masters from the countryside. In Brazil, the emancipationists had hoped that abolition would be accompanied by land reform, political inclusion and the creation of a more equal society. None of this happened. In 1889 the monarchy was overthrown by a military coup, supported by former slave holding elites who consolidated their domination over the rest of Brazilian society for the next half-century. The hopes for a much more radical transformation of the empire were stillborn as a result of the coup and the vast inequalities that characterized Brazilian society of the colonial and imperial periods continued into the republican era. Nevertheless, the ending of servile labour in both empires was a transformative moment, when millions of people ceased to be things and were recognized as human beings.

The emancipation of serfs and slaves in Russia and Brazil was a multi-faceted process which spanned decades, if not centuries. At its heart was the refusal of the oppressed bondsmen to accept their lot, something that has been common to every form of coerced labour. The refusal to internalize and legitimize the existing state of affairs created a constant tension within servile societies no matter how docile or calm the enserfed and enslaved seemed. Serf and slave resistance was a continual threat to the established order. However, on its own, it rarely possessed the strength to overthrow the existing order. To achieve abolition support was needed beyond the servile community. An intellectual and moral climate had to exist in which servile labour was seen as a gross affront to human dignity, but changed intellectual and moral attitudes were not enough to abolish servile labour. The power of the master-class was inseparably entwined with the economic, social and political structures in the two empires and that class fiercely defended its rights to ownership of other human beings. Opposition from the oppressed themselves and the intellectual and moral delegitimization of slavery and serfdom combined to put both systems under threat. However, in themselves, they were not sufficient to bring about emancipation. For that a third stage was necessary – a political one.

The shift of emancipation onto a new field of battle, a political one, began in the last quarter of the eighteenth century and rapidly gained momentum. The Revolutionary and Napoleonic wars contributed substantially to the abolition of slavery and serfdom in Europe and the Americas, both intentionally and indirectly. The conversion of Britain, the most powerful state in the world, to the anti-slavery cause marked a turning point in the fight for abolition. Yet at the end of the Napoleonic Wars slavery and serfdom remained intact and even continued to grow. In the Russian Empire, serfdom survived the wars unscathed and in Brazil, a coffee boom led to a substantial expansion of slavery. In neither empire did the leadership possess the political will to take on the issue of emancipation. In Russia Alexander I and Nicholas I both thought seriously about emancipation, but shrank from the decisive action necessary to achieve this aim. Dom Pedro I and his son Dom Pedro II similarly opposed slavery, but recognized that there was no possibility of abolition under the circumstances prevailing in the first half of the nineteenth century.

Those circumstances changed as servile systems marked the countries that had them as pariah states. Claims to a place among the civilized nations of the world could not be entertained while servile labour existed. For the political elites at the highest level of the two empires, this dilemma became more acute as the decades passed. Still absent, however, was the political will to bring about emancipation. What was necessary was a crisis of sufficient magnitude to galvanize the political will to bring about emancipation. In both cases, war was the first stimulant to political action. A disastrous defeat in the Crimean War for Russia and an exhausting victory for Brazil in the Paraguayan War spurred Alexander II and Dom Pedro II to confront the question of servile labour directly. That political battle would be fought out in political systems that were either dominated by the emperor as in the Russian case or in which the emperor was the most significant player as in the Brazilian case. The initiative of the monarch to initiate, support or to terminate the movement for emancipation was critical.

This was the context in which the two princesses, Elena and Isabel, became active participants in the struggle for emancipation. Both women were close to the source of political power, the emperors, and in Isabel's case she temporarily possessed that power. They used their position to not only to drive forward the emancipation project in general, but also to shape the form that that emancipation took. Both women had to contend with an environment that was actively hostile to women's participation in public life and was becoming more so as the century progressed. Beyond the general hostility, the issue of emancipation was the most politically taboo matter in both empires. That the two women chose to intervene on this issue was not a coincidence. Morality was the sphere assigned to women under the prevailing patriarchal ideology and for hundreds of thousands of women, slavery was a moral issue. Removing it, however, was a political issue. Emancipation blurred that distinction, allowing women to participate in the wider struggle. By the mid-nineteenth century, women had become the backbone of the anti-slavery movement. This moral/political dichotomy also drove the action of both Elena and Isabel.

Both women regarded emancipation as a great moral crusade. Their frequent statements linking morality and emancipation leave no doubt that morality was the basis of their actions. But that should not allow us to relegate their actions to an unthreatening, neutered moral sphere. Outraged morality is neither safe nor conservative. Neither woman was naíve nor inexperienced in political matters; both were hardened politicians. Elena had spent over thirty years at the Russian Court and was an expert in its workings, particularly its hidden ones. Isabel at the time of her third regency was an experienced, not to say bruised, politician. The two princesses also possessed determination, drive and a real sense of purpose. They were politically astute, capable of running risks and did not lack courage. In short, they had opportunity, the motive and the political nous to make the most of the situation they found themselves in. Recognizing their role in the respective emancipations does not diminish the role of other actors or other causes, but it does increase our understanding of this complex and many-tiered process.

It also, however, speaks to a larger question of women and power and the ways in which contemporaries and historians view such women. Vilification, denial or neutering of such women enables them to be incorporated into traditional narratives of male and female, public and private, active and passive. Royal women by their very nature never fitted neatly into these categories. The space that this created between ideology and necessity allowed those royal women with sufficient desire and intelligence the opportunity to play a much more active role in the public life of the state. The reluctance to accept these women as political actors plays to conventions about acceptable behaviour and roles. At times, the women themselves actively cooperated in downplaying their own actions so as ruffle fewer feathers. But this should not disguise the fact that these royal women were formidable politicians and were capable of the most consequential interventions. The emancipations in the empires of Russia and Brazil are an enduring testimony to their influence.

BIBLIOGRAPHY

Archival Source

Petrópolis Arquivo Grão Pará
Petrópolis Arquivo da Casa Imperial do Brasil

Published Sources in Portuguese

Revista Illustrada
Gazeta da Tarde
Extinção da Escravidão do Brasil. Discussão na Camara dos Deputados u no Senado (Rio de Janeiro, 1889).
Falas do Trono de Dom Pedro I, Dom Pedro II e Princesa Isabel (Brasília, 2019).
Império Brasileiro: Falas do Trono desde o Ano de 1823 até o Ano de 1889 (Brasília, 1977).
Cabral de Mello, E. (ed), *Joaquim Nabuco Essencial* (São Paulo, 2010).
Caldeira, J. (ed), *José Bonifácio de Andrade e Silva* (São Paulo, 2002).
Flora, A. and I.I. Verissimo (eds), *André Rebouças: Diário e Notas Autobiográficas* (Rio de Janeiro, 1938).
Kann, B. (ed), *D. Leopoldina: Cartas de Uma Imperatriz* (São Paulo, 2006).
Nogueira, O. (ed), *Constituições Brasileiras* (3rd ed, Brasília, 2012).
Patrocínio, J., *Campanha abolicionista: coletânea de artigos* (Rio de Janeiro, 1996).
Sobrinho, B. (ed), *Antonio da Silva Jardim. Propaganda Republicana (1888–1889). Discursos, Opusculos, Manifestos e Artigos Coligidos* (Rio de Janeiro, 1978).

Published Sources in Russian

Russkaia Starina
Russkii Archiv
Svod ZakonovRossiiskoi Imperii (32 vols, St. Petersburg, 1857).
Empress Catherine II, *Zapiski Imperatritsy Ekateriny Velikoi* (St. Petersburg, 1907).
Fedorov, V.A. (ed), *Konets Krepostnichestva v Rossii: Dokumenty, Pis'ma, Memuary, Stat'i* (Moscow, 1994).
'Zaveshchanie Imperatritsy Marii Fedorovny', *Russkaia Starina*, 33 (1882).
Korf, M.A., *Zapiski* (Moscow, 2003).
———, *Dnevnik God 1843-I* (Moscow, 2004).
———, *Dnevniki 1838 i 1839 gg.* (Moscow, 2010).
Miliutin, D.A., *Vospominaniia General-Fel'dmarshala Grafa Dmitriia Alekseevicha Miliutina 1868-nachalo 1873* (Moscow, 2006).

Miliutina, M.A., 'Iz Zapisok Marii Ageevny Miliutinoi', *Russkaia Starina*, 97, 98 (1889).
Mironenko, S.V. (ed), *Dnevniki Velikogo Kniazia Konstantina Nikolaevicha. 1858–1864* (Moscow, 2019).
Mrochkovskaia-Balashova, S. (ed), *Dolli Fikel'mon: Dnevnik 1829–1837 Bce Pushkinskii Peterburg* (Moscow, 2009).
Obolenskii, D., 'Moi Vospominaniia', *Russkaia Starina*, 137, 143 (1909).
Rubenstein, A., 'Vospominaniia Antona Grigorovicha Rubensteina', *Russkaia Starina*, 64 (1889).
Semenov, Tian-Shanskii P., *Memuary* (5 vols, Moscow, 2018).
Solov'ev, D.V. (ed), *Elizaveta i Aleksandr: Khronika po pis'mam Imperatritsy Elizavety Alekseevny 1792–1826* (Moscow, 2013).
Tiutcheva, A., *Vospominaniia: Pri Dvore dvukh Imperaterov* (Moscow, 2008).
Trubetskaia, O. (ed), *Materialy dlia Biografii kn. V.A. Cherkasskogo* (2 vols, St. Petersburg, 1901).

Published Sources in English

Ewbank, T., *Life in Brazil or a Journal of a Visit to the Land of the Cocoa and the Palm* (New York, 1856).
Hayward, J. and Caballero, M. (eds), *Maria Graham's Journal of a Voyage to Brazil* (Anderson, 2010).
Jackman, S.W., *Romanov Relations: The Private Correspondence of Tsars Alexander I, Nicholas I and the Grand Dukes Constantine and Michael with their Sister Queen Anna Pavlovna* (London, 1969).
Koster, H., *Travels in Brazil* (London, 1816).
Kropotkin, P., *Memoirs of a Revolution*ist (New York, 1971).
McKay, J. (ed), *Four Russian Serf Narratives* (Madison, WI, 2010).
Parthé, K. (ed), *A Herzen Reader* (Evanston, IL, 2012).
Rieber, A., *The Politics of the Autocracy: Letters of Alexander II to Prince A.I Bariatinskii* (The Hague, 1966).
Thaler, R.P., *Alexander Nikolaevich Radishchev: A Journey from St. Petersburg to Moscow* (Cambridge, MA, 1958).

Secondary Works in Portuguese

Azevedo, F.L. Nogueria de., *Carlota Joaquina na Corte do Brasil* (Rio de Janeiro, 2003).
Barra, S., *Entre a Corte e a Cidade: O Rio de Janeiro no Tempo do Rei (1808–1821)* (Rio de Janeiro, 2008).
Calmon, P., *A Princesa Isabel 'A Redentora'* (São Paulo, 1941).
Carvalho, J. Murilo de., *A Construção da Ordem: Teatro de Sombras* (Rio de Janeiro, 2003).
———, *D. Pedro II* (São Paulo, 2007).
———, *Os Bestializados: O Rio de Janeiro e a República que não foi* (São Paulo, 2011).
Chalhoub, S., *Visões da Liberdade: Uma História das Últimas Décadas da Escravidão na Corte* (São Paulo, 1990).
———, *A Força da Escravidão: Ilegalidade e Costume no Brasil Oitocentista* (São Paulo, 2012).
Costa, E.V., *A Abolição* (8th edition, revised and expanded, São Paulo, 2008).
Daibert, R., *Isabel: A 'Redentora' dos Escravos* (São Paulo, 2004).
Del Priore, M., *O Castelo de Papel* (Rio de Janeiro, 2013).

Dolhnikoff, M., *O Pacto Imperial: Origens do Federalismo no Brasil* (São Paulo, 2005).
Doratioto, F., *Maldita Guerra: Nova História da Guerra do Paraguai* (São Paulo, 2002).
Freyre, G., *Casa Grande i Senzala: Formação da Família Brasileira sob o Regime da Economia Patriarchal* (Rio de Janeiro, 1933).
Gomes, F. dos Santos., *Histórias de Quilombolas: Mocambos e Comunidades de Senzalas no Rio de Janeiro, Século XIX* (São Paulo, 2006).
Lacombe, L.L., *Isabel A Princesa Redentora: Biografia baseada em Documentos Inêditos* (Petrópolis, 1989).
Nabuco, C.A., 'Redentora e os Abolicionistas', *Revista Instituto Histórico e Geográfico Brasileiro*, 192 (1946).
Parron, T., *A Política da Escravidão no Império do Brasil* (Rio de Janeiro, 2011).
Pedreira, J. and F.D. Costa, *Dom João VI: Um Príncipe entre Dois Continentes* (São Paulo, 2008).
Reis, J.J., *Rebelião Escrava no Brasil: A História do Levante dos Malês em 1835* (revised and expanded edition, São Paulo, 2003).
Soares, L.C., *O 'Povo de Cam' na Capital do Brasil: A Escravidão Urbana no Rio de Janeiro de Século XIX* (Rio de Janeiro, 2007).
Schwarcz, L.M., *As Barbas do Imperador: Dom Pedro II, Um Monarca nos Trópicos* (2nd ed, São Paulo, 2010).
Schwarcz, L.M. and H.M. Starling., *Brasil: Uma Biografia* (São Paulo, 2015).
Silva E. (São Paulo, 2003).
Viana, Maria de Lourdes., 'Isabel de Bragança: Uma Princesa Imperial', *Revista Instituto Histórico e Geográfico Brasileiro*, 158 (1997).

Secondary Works in Russian

Anonymous, 'Velikaia Kniaginia Elena Pavlovna, 1806–1873', *Russkaia Starina*, 33 (1882).
Arsen'ev, D.S., *Zhizneopisanie Imperatritsy Marii Aleksandrovny 1838–1854* (Moscow, 2018).
Bazhenova, O.K. (ed), *Velikaia Kniaginia Elena Pavlovna* (St. Petersburg, 2011).
Beliakov, N.A. and V.A. Mikhailovich, 'Krestovozdvizhenskaia Obshchina', in Bazhenova, (ed), *Velikaia Kniaginia Elena Pavlovna* (St. Petersburg, 2011).
Bakhrushin, S.V., 'Velikaia Kniaginia Elena Pavlovna', in *Osvobozhdenie Krest'ian: Deiateli Reformy* (Moscow, 1911).
Bukh, K.D., 'Velikaia Kniaginia Elena Pavlovna', *Russkaia Starina*, 57 (1888).
Dzhanshiev, G.A., *Epokha Velikikh Reform* (St. Petersburg, 2016).
Druzhinin, N.M., *Russkaia Derevnia na Perelome 1861–1880* gg. (Moscow, 1978).
Ivanova, N.A. and V.P. Zheltova, *Soslovnoe Obshchestvo Rossiiskoi Imperii* (Moscow, 2019).
Komissarov, B.N. and S.G. Bozhkova, *F.F. Borel' Pervyi Rossiiskii Poslannik v Brazilii* (St. Petersburg, 2000).
Koni, A.F., 'Velikaia Kniaginia Elena Pavlovna', in S.A. Vengerov (ed), *Glavnye Deiateli osvobozhdeniia krest'ian* (St. Petersburg, 1903).
Ponomareva, V.V. and L.B. Khoroshilova, *Mir Russkoi Zhenshchiny: Sem'ia, Professiia, Domashnii Uklad XVIII – Nachalo XX veka* (Moscow, 2016).
Reznikova, E.E., 'Rol' Velikoi Kniagini Eleny Pavlovny v politicheskoi zhizni Rossii', in Bazhenova (ed), *Velikaia Kniaginia Elena Pavlovna* (St. Petersburg, 2011).
Semevskii, V. 'Krepostnye Krest'iane pri Eklaterine II', *Russkaia Starina*, 17 (1876).
Shevchenko, M.M., *Istoriia Krepostnogo Prava v Rossii* (Voronezh, 1981).

Shil'der, N.K., *Imperator Aleksandr Pervyi: Ero zhizn i tsarstvovanie* (4 vols, St. Petersburg, 1904).
Sidorova, A., *Obrazovat' v detiakh um, serdtse i dushu: Vospitanie Velikikh Kniazei v Sem'iakh Imperaterov Nikolaia I i Alexandra II* (Moscow, 2019).
Studenkin, G.I., 'Saltychika 1730–1801', *Russkaia Starina*, 10, 1874.
Tatishchev, S.S., *Imperator Aleksandr II: Ego Zhizn' i Tsarstvovanie* (2 vols, St. Petersburg, 1903).
Zablotskii, A.P., *Graf P.D.Kiselev e ero Vremia: Materialy dlia Istorii Imperatorov Aleksandra I, Nikolaia I i Aleksandra II* (4 vols, St. Petersburg, 1882).
Zaionchkovskii, P.A., *Otmena Krepostnogo Prava v Rossii* (Moscow, 1968).
Zav'ialova, L. and Kirill Orlov, *Velikii Kniaz' Konstantin Nikolaevich i Velikie Kniaz'ia Konstantinovichi: Istoriia Sem'i* (St. Petersburg, 2009).
Zav'ialova, L., *Maria Fedorovna: Zhena, Mat', Imperatritsa* (St. Petersburg, 2018).
Zhakarova, L.G., *Samoderzhavie i Otmena Krepostnogo Prava v Rossi 1856–1861* (Moscow, 1984).
———, *Aleksandr II i Otmena Krepostnogo Prava v Rossii* (Moscow, 2011).
Zimin, I.V., *Tsarskaia Rabota XIX-Nachalo XX Veka: Povsednevnaia Zhizn' Rossiiskogo Imperatorskogo Dvora* (St. Petersburg, 2011).
———, *Povsednevnaia Zhizn' Rossiiskogo Imperatorskogo Dvora Vtoraia Chervert XIX-Nachalo XX v.: Vzroslyi Mir Imperatorskikh Rezidentsii* (St. Petersburg, 2010).

Secondary Works in English

Alexander, J.T., *Catherine the Great: Life and Legend* (Oxford, 1989).
Antonova, K.P., *An Ordinary Marriage: The World of a Gentry Family in Provincial Russia* (Oxford, 2013).
Barman, R.J., *Citizen Emperor: Pedro II and the Making of Brazil, 1825–91* (Stanford, 1999).
———, *Princess Isabel of Brazil: Gender and Power in the Nineteenth Century* (Willington, 2002).
Bartley, P., *Queen Victoria* (|Abingdon, 2016).
Berdayev, N., *The Origins of Russian Communism* (Michigan, 1970).
Bethell, L., *The Abolition of the Brazilian Slave Trade* (Cambridge, 1970).
Blum, J., *Lord and Peasant in Russia from the Ninth to the Nineteenth Century* (Princeton, 1961).
Brown, C., *Moral Capital: Foundations of British Abolitionism* (Chapel Hill, 2006).
Bush, M.L., *Servitude in Modern Times* (Cambridge, 2000).
———, *Serfdom and Slavery: Studies in Legal Bondage* (London, 2015).
Bushkovitch, P., *Peter the Great: The Struggle for Power, 1671–1725* (Cambridge, 2001).
Campbell, R., *Seneca: Letters from a Stoic* (London, 2014).
Clark, C., *The Iron Kingdom: The Rise and Downfall of Prussia 1600–1947* (London, 2006).
Conrad, R., *The Destruction of Brazilian Slavery* (Berkeley, 1972).
Cowling, C., *Conceiving Freedom: Women of Color, Gender and the Abolition of Slavery in Havana and Rio de Janeiro* (Chapel Hill, 2013).
Davis, D.B., *Inhuman Bondage:The Rise and Fall of Slavery in the New World* (Oxford, 2006).
Domar, E., *Capitalism, Socialism and Serfdom* (Cambridge, 1989).
Drescher, S., *Abolition: A History of Slavery and Anti-Slavery* (Cambridge, 2009).
Eltis, D., S. Engerman, S. Drescher, D. Richardson (eds), *The Cambridge World History of Slavery: Volume 4, AD 1804–AD 2016* (Cambridge, 2017).
Etkind, A., *Internal Colonization: Russia's Imperial Experience* (Cambridge, 2011).
Evans, B.E., *Bolshevik Women* (Cambridge, 1997).
Field, D., *The End of Russian Serfdom: Nobility and Bureaucracy in Russia, 1855–1861* (Cambridge, MA, 1976).

Fuchs, R.G. and V.E. Thompson, *Women in Nineteenth Century Europe* (Basingstoke, 2010).
Graham, R., *Patronage and Politics in Nineteenth Century Brazil* (Stanford, 1990).
Graham, S., *House and Street: The Domestic World of Servants and Masters in Nineteenth Century Rio de Janeiro* (Cambridge, 1995).
Hellie, R., *Slavery in Russia 1450–1725* (Chicago, 1982).
Jeffrey, J.R., *The Great Silent Army of Abolitionism: Ordinary Women in the Anti-Slavery Movement* (Chapel Hill, 1998).
Kittelson, R.A., *The Practice of Politics in Postcolonial Brazil: Porto Alegre, 1845–1895* (Pittsburgh, 2006).
Klein, H.S. and F.V. Luna, *Slavery in Brazil* (Cambridge, 2010).
Klein, H.S. and Ben Vinson, *African Slavery in Latin America and the Caribbean* (2nd ed. Cambridge, 2007).
Kolchin, S., *Unfree Labour: American Slavery and Russian Serfdom* (Boston, 1990).
Lincoln, W.B., 'The Karlovka Reform', *Slavic Review*, 28 (1969).
———, 'The Circle of Grand Duchess Elena Pavlovna,' 1848–1861' *Slavonic and East European Review*, 48 (1970).
———, *In the Vanguard of Reform: Russia's Enlightened Bureaucrats, 1825–1861* (Dekalb, IL, 1992).
Mattoso, K.M., *To Be a Slave in Brazil 1550–1888* (Rutgers, 1986).
McGrew, R., *Paul I of Russia 1754–1801* (Oxford, 1992).
McKay, J. (ed), *Four Russian Serf Narratives* (Madison, WI, 2009).
Midgley, C., *Women against Slavery: The British Campaigns 1780–1870* (London, 1992).
Moon, D., *The Abolition of Serfdom in Russia, 1762–1907* (Harlow, 2001).
Needle, J., *The Party of Order: The Conservatives, The State and Slavery in the Brazilian Monarchy 1831–1871* (Stanford Press, 2006).
O'Rourke, S., 'The Mother Benefactress and the Sacred Battalion: Grand Duchess Elena Pavlovna, the Editing Commission and the Emancipation of the Serfs', *The Russian Review*, 70 (2011).
———, 'Monarchy, Gender, and Emancipation: Grand Duchess Elena Pavlovna of Russia and Princess Isabel of Brazil and the Ending of Servile Labour', *Slavery and Abolition*, 35 (2014).
———, 'The Emancipation of the Serfs in Europe', in Eltis et al. (eds), *The Cambridge World History of Slavery*, vol. 4 (Cambridge, 2017).
Paquette, G., *Imperial Portugal in the Age of Atlantic Revolutions: The Luso-Brazilian World, c. 1770–1850* (Cambridge, 2013).
Read, I., *The Hierarchies of Slavery in Santos, Brazil 1822–1888* (Stanford, 2012).
Rey, M.-P., *Alexander I: The Tsar Who Defeated Napoleon* (Dekalb, IL, 2012).
Russell-Wood, A.J., *Slavery and Freedom in Colonial Brazil* (Oxford, 2002).
Schwartz, S.B., *Sugar Plantations in the Formation of Brazilian Society Bahia, 1550–1835* (Cambridge, 1985).
———, *Slaves, Peasants and Rebels: Reconsidering Brazlian Slavery* (Urbana, IL, 1996).
Scott, J.C., *The Moral Economy of the Peasant: Rebellion and Subsistence in Southeast Asia* (New Haven, 1976).
Soraka, M. and C. Ruud, *Becoming a Romanov: Grand Duchess Elena of Russia and Her World (1807–1873)* (Farnham, 2015).
Stites, R., *Serfdom, Society and the Arts in Imperial Russia: The Pleasure and the Power* (Princeton, 2005).

Taylor, M., *The Interest: How the British Establishment Resisted the Abolition of Slavery* (London, 2020).

Thyrêt, I., *Between God and the Tsar: Religious Symbolism and the Royal Women of Muscovite Russia* (Dekalb, IL, 2001).

Wcislo, F.W., *Reforming Rural Russia: State, Local Society, and National Politics 1855–1914* (Princeton, 1990).

Wilentz, S. (ed), *Rites of Power: Symbolism, Ritual and Politics since the Middle Ages* (Philadelphia, 1999).

Wortman, R., *Scenarios of Power: Myth and Ceremony in Russian Monarchy* (2 vols, Princeton, 1995 and 2000).

INDEX

Milton Keynes UK
Ingram Content Group UK Ltd.
UKHW011015220823
427243UK00002BA/206